101 Questions & Answers on CATHOLICISM AND EVOLUTION

101 Questions & Answers on CATHOLICISM AND EVOLUTION

Louis M. Savary

Paulist Press
New York / Mahwah, NJ

Scripture quotations are from New Revised Standard Version Bible: Catholic Edition, copyright © 1989, 1993 National Council of the Churches of Christ in the United States of America. Used by permission. All rights reserved worldwide.

Cover image by bepsy / Shutterstock.com
Cover and book design by Lynn Else

Library of Congress Cataloging-in-Publication Data
Names: Savary, Louis M., author.
Title: 101 questions & answers on Catholicism and evolution / Louis M. Savary.
Other titles: 101 questions and answers on Catholicism and evolution
Description: Paperback. | New York, Mahwah NJ: Paulist Press, [2024] | Series: 101 questions & answers on | Includes bibliographical references. | Summary: "Using the format of questions and answers, this book presents the history of the Catholic Church's relationship to science, specifically evolution, information on evolution itself, and, drawing on the writings of Pierre Teilhard de Chardin, discussion of Christianity as an evolutionary religion and what that implies for its future"—Provided by publisher.
Identifiers: LCCN 2023053747 (print) | LCCN 2023053748 (ebook) | ISBN 9780809157099 (paperback) | ISBN 9780809188642 (ebook)
Subjects: LCSH: Evolution—Religious aspects—Catholic Church—Miscellanea. | Catholic Church—Doctrines—Miscellanea.
Classification: LCC BX1795.E85 S37 2024 (print) | LCC BX1795.E85 (ebook) | DDC 233/.11—dc23/eng/20240331
LC record available at https://lccn.loc.gov/2023053747
LC ebook record available at https://lccn.loc.gov/2023053748

ISBN 978-0-8091-5709-9 (paperback)
ISBN 978-0-8091-8864-2 (e-book)

Published by Paulist Press
997 Macarthur Boulevard
Mahwah, New Jersey 07430
www.paulistpress.com

Printed and bound in the
United States of America

Contents

Preface

Charles Darwin's *On the Origin of Species*, published in 1859, shocked the Christian world. Its factual evidence challenged the biblical foundations of Christianity and the traditional understanding of Earth's story. Christian churches—all of them—felt threatened by the unsettling details in Darwin's book. Illustrations on its pages showed that almost all species of plants and animals on Earth today evolved from earlier species. More unsettling to many believers, the emerging pattern suggested that human beings most likely evolved biologically from primates.

As Darwin's book became well known, many churches officially and publicly denied and decried the "theory" of evolution. Many religious leaders declined even to look at and examine what they were denying. Not only did they refuse to see what might be true and real, they also chose *not* to see it. Implicitly, they were also telling the faithful to do the same. Their only reason: because evolution appeared to contradict the "word of God" in the Bible.

Consequently, since the late nineteenth century, Christians have remained wary of even mentioning the word *evolution*. Few church officials in the nineteenth and early twentieth century believed that the Bible and evolution could ever be reconciled.

Darwin's book shook up the scientific world too. Scientists did not initially welcome the discovery of evolution. They had never had to deal with a concept as fundamentally new and challenging. Before the mid-nineteenth century, very few scientists gave thought to the idea of evolution. Many had no idea evolution was a reality. That all changed with the 1859 publication of Darwin's book. At first, even biologists reacted negatively and fearfully toward evolution, much as officials in the church did. Most laypeople remained unaware of this crisis within the scientific community. Slowly, evolution, in theory and practice, came to be accepted by scientists. In time, evolutionary theory became a foundational principle of the biological sciences. Later, scientists in other fields began recognizing evolution happening in their domains as well.

By the 1920s, chapters on evolution began appearing in American public high school biology textbooks. Today, every student studying biology is familiar with the principles of evolution. Yet many people of faith, especially clergy, are still afraid to discuss evolution publicly or even say the word aloud. Consequently, many believers hesitate to inquire about the topic and how it relates to their faith. They may have questions about it but are usually afraid to ask them.

Early in the twentieth century, state governments were concerned about the scientific acceptance of evolution, especially in places where most voters were Bible-reading Christians. These states enacted protective laws prohibiting science teachers from discussing evolution in their classrooms, even when biology textbooks contained chapters on evolution. Challenges to overturn such laws failed, inspiring many more states to pass similar prohibitions. In a few states, such laws forbidding the teaching of evolution remained on the books until the mid-1960s.

As long as people, especially Christians, remain ignorant of evolution and its unavoidable presence and significance, they will remain fearful of it and avoid learning about it. I hope to deal with most if not all the problems theologians and scriptural literalists have with the issue.

A question-and-answer format enables simple and clear responses to many of the questions people of faith typically have about evolution but don't know how to ask. I hope to explain to the ordinary reader the evolutionary process and how it relates to Christian faith, daily work, spirituality, and spiritual practice.

In part 1, I begin with basic and familiar theological and scriptural questions related to evolution.

In part 2, I answer questions about evolution itself and how it works.

In part 3, I show how Christianity has always contributed to human evolution.

In part 4, I deal with questions about Christianity's possible evolutionary future.

The first questions that most people ask have very simple answers:

- *Should a Christian be afraid to study evolution?*

  No. The Catholic Church and many other Christian denominations no longer prohibit the study of evolution.
- *Does evolution contradict the Bible?*

  No. Not as long as you don't require the biblical text to qualify as an up-to-date scientific and historically accurate document.
- *Who was the first person to show how Christianity and evolution could be reconciled?*

  The first person to integrate modern science and evolution with Christian theology was a French Jesuit scientist, Pierre Teilhard de Chardin, SJ (1881–1955). A well-known geologist and paleontologist, he published over 1,500 scientific articles. Teilhard was part of the geological team that discovered Peking Man, one of the evolutionary precursors of *Homo sapiens*. The church silenced him for writing about evolution and its prevalence in the universe.

  It was only after his death in 1955 that his books and essays became available. People soon begin to learn of his original insights that explained how evolution may enrich our understanding of Christian theology. We will be learning many of Teilhard de Chardin's ideas in this book.

- *Can the study of evolution help us better understand God's ways?*

  I hope to show that it can.

PART 1

CATHOLICISM'S GRADUAL ACCEPTANCE OF EVOLUTION

Despite the remarkable achievements in research science in the twentieth century, the majority of Americans do not know much about the science of evolution, nor do they know the difference between evolution, intelligent design and creationism.

Sr. Ilia Delio, OSF[1]

The Church's Changing Position on Evolution

1. When was evolution first officially acknowledged by the Catholic Church?

The official church acknowledged the theory of evolution in 1950. Pope Pius XII (papacy 1939–58) was the first pope to directly address the issue of evolution in his 1950 encyclical *Humani Generis*. This document stated that nothing in Catholic doctrine is contradicted by a theory that suggests one species might evolve into another, even if that species is *Homo sapiens*. Here is a quote from the encyclical:

> The Teaching Authority of the Church does not forbid that, in conformity with the present state of human sciences and sacred theology, research and discussions, on the part of men experienced in both fields, take place with regard to the doctrine of evolution, in as far as it inquires into the origin of the human body as coming from pre-existent and living matter—for the Catholic faith obliges us to hold that souls are immediately created by God.[2]

Surprisingly, even today, over seventy-five years later, the Catholic Church rarely uses the word *evolution* in its public statements. Evolution is seldom if ever talked about from the pulpit and is not discussed in the official *Catechism of the Catholic Church*.

2. Why doesn't the Catholic Church talk about evolution?

There is no simple answer to this question.

One likely reason for the hesitancy is that *most clergy don't understand evolutionary processes*. Therefore, they hesitate to speak from the pulpit about a principle of science they don't understand. The few who are knowledgeable about evolution avoid the topic because it remains controversial. They prefer to keep science and religion separate. It's easier that way.

Another reason is that evolution would challenge the church and clergy *to explain to the faithful why the Bible is not historically and scientifically accurate.* Bishops and priests fear, probably rightly so, that discussing evolution from the pulpit would prove confusing to many less-scientifically educated believers. Clergy also fear that it would be upsetting for parishioners to hear them acknowledge that the Bible is the "word of God," yet might not be historically and scientifically accurate.

For example, in the first chapter in the Book of Genesis, the Bible says that God created the world in six days. Yet science assures us that the universe is over thirteen billion years old. Also in Genesis 2, the Bible says that God created human beings directly from the dust of the earth, yet science offers evidence that we evolved over millions of years, emerging from primate and hominid evolutionary lines. This gradual emergence implies that our human species descended from the giant apes and earlier hominids. One can't expect a preacher to adequately deal with those two issues in a ten-minute sermon.

3. Why do many Catholics avoid talking about evolution?

Here are four reasons for this hesitancy:

One is because most Catholics do not understand evolutionary processes.

Another is that Catholics are generally reluctant, or even afraid, to publicly discuss a topic that might threaten their religious beliefs.

A third reason Catholics hesitate to talk about evolution is that the church publicly has remained silent about the topic. Priests do not mention it from the pulpit, nor is it discussed in religious education classes, even in classes for adult catechumens. The unspoken message is that it is inappropriate or even dangerous to talk about it.

Moreover, the *Catechism of the Catholic Church*, originally published in 1983, does not discuss evolution or present any official church position regarding it. The word *evolution* is not even listed in the *Catechism*'s index. Nor does the revised edition's index include it. So, if someone looked to the *Catechism* to find out what the church teaches about evolution, they would find no answer.

A fourth reason, discussed more fully later, is that early in the twentieth century the Catholic Church in Rome explicitly ordered its philosophers and theologians to take an oath against "modernism." Although *modernism* was a vague term, clearly the popes meant "modern science and evolutionary theory."

This "oath" has had longstanding negative effects, discouraging Catholic scientists, philosophers, and theologians from the study of evolution.

4. What is "theistic evolution"?

Theistic evolution is not a single scientific theory, but rather "a range of views about how the science of evolution generally relates to religious beliefs." It is an inclusive term used to describe several viewpoints. These viewpoints all agree on two statements: (1) they accept evolution as a scientific theory, and (2) they see no reason why God could not have used a natural evolutionary process in forming the human species.[3] These various "theistic" perspectives consider "religious teachings about God as compatible with modern scientific understanding about biological evolution."[4] The theistic evolution viewpoint marks a great advance from those who want to keep science and religion separate. Theistic evolution *integrates* science and evolution.

For example, Francis Collins, MD, is a famous American physician-geneticist and a devout Christian. He holds a theistic evolutionary view that he explained in a popular book called *The Language of God: A Scientist Presents Evidence for Belief.*[5]

Collins believes that "evolution is real, but that it was set in motion by God." He characterizes it as accepting "that evolution occurred as biologists describe it, but under the direction of God."[6]

Among his scientific achievements, Collins discovered the genes associated with a number of diseases. He also led the Human Genome Project, whose challenging objective was to map the entire human genome. Thanks to this map, today ordinary people for a small fee can now get a report on their own DNA, track their personal ancestry, and find others genetically related to them. Collins also formerly directed the National Institutes of Health (NIH) in Bethesda, Maryland.

Because we don't find a discussion of this question in the *Catechism*, we must look to what some of the more recent popes have said about it. From their words, it is safe to say that the Catholic Church today accepts what might be called "theistic evolution."

5. What have popes since Vatican II (1962–65) said about evolution?

Pope St. John XXIII (papacy 1958–63) convened the ecumenical council, Vatican II, because he felt the church needed to catch up with the modern world. He used the Italian word *aggiornamento*, which means "bringing up to date." Perhaps, the most important *aggiornamento* document the council published in this regard was called Pastoral Constitution on the Church in the Modern World (*Gaudium et Spes*).

The documents of Vatican II, published in the mid-1960s, were written before there were any significant favorable papal pronouncements on evolution. One looks in vain for an explicit discussion or even mention of evolution in any of its documents.[7]

However, the "spirit of evolution" was clearly in the air during that ecumenical council.[8] For example, the Pastoral Constitution on the Church in the Modern World states:

> May the faithful, therefore, live in very close union with the other men of their time and may they strive to understand perfectly their way of thinking and judging, as expressed in their culture. Let them blend new sciences and theories and the understanding of the most recent discoveries with Christian morality and the teaching of Christian doctrine, so that their religious culture and morality may keep pace with scientific knowledge and with the constantly progressing technology. Thus they will be able to interpret and evaluate all things in a truly Christian spirit. (64)

6. What did Pope St. John Paul II (papacy 1978–2005) add to the discussion?

Pope St. John Paul II visited the question of evolution in a 1996 message to the Pontifical Academy of Sciences.[9] He acknowledged witnessing many changes in the church's approach to evolution since *Humani Generis* (1950).

John Paul II recognized that the theory of evolution was more than just a clever idea or a hypothesis. He also recognized that this theory was now accepted by scientists and validated by research, and that evolutionary theory was also being applied to various fields of knowledge, not merely biology. He observed that many different fields were independently conducting experiments that seemed to confirm evolutionary theory, "a significant argument in favor of the theory."[10]

Evolution, Pope John Paul II said, is "an essential subject which deeply interests the Church." He recognized that science and scripture sometimes have "apparent contradictions," but said that when this is the case, a "solution" must be found because "truth cannot contradict truth."

Notice that in this speech the pope was talking only to an exclusive group of scientists, not to a general audience.

John Paul II also acknowledged that a variety of new scientific discoveries could provide examples of how science might inspire the Church to seek a new and "correct interpretation of the inspired word."[11] Scripture scholars today commonly use scientific analytic techniques to interpret literary forms, literary usage, translations, and document dating more accurately.

However, very few of these positive ideas on evolution made their way into the pope's sermons or public speeches.

7. What has Pope Francis added to the discussion?

Before Pope Francis (papacy 2013–) became a Jesuit and a theologian, he had been a scientist, a chemist, who was quite familiar with the theory of evolution. In a papal message delivered to the Pontifical Academy of Sciences in 2014, he said:

> When we read the account of Creation in Genesis we risk imagining that God was a magician, complete with an all powerful magic wand. But that was not so. He created beings and he let them develop according to the internal laws with which He endowed each one.... The Big Bang theory, which is proposed today as the origin of the world, does not contradict the intervention of a divine creator but depends on it. Evolution in nature does not conflict with the notion of Creation, because evolution presupposes the creation of beings who evolve.[12]

Once again, the pope was speaking only to an exclusive group of professional scientists, not to the public. This message was never passed on to the faithful in the pews by the local clergy.

The *Catechism of the Catholic Church* indirectly supports Pope Francis's perspective, but carefully avoids the term *evolution*. Instead, it pictures the universe on a "journey" to its destiny.

Creation has its own goodness and proper perfection, but it did not spring forth complete from the hands of the Creator. The universe was created "in a state of journeying" (*in statu viae*) toward an ultimate perfection yet to be attained, to which God has destined it.[13]

8. What does the Catholic Church say about evolution today?

Unfortunately, even textual revisions of the *Catechism of the Catholic Church* do not deal explicitly with evolution. The text seems to carefully avoid using the word *evolution*, while it acknowledges that science can contribute to our understanding of creation. Scientific discoveries, it says, "have splendidly enriched our knowledge of the age and dimensions of the cosmos, the development of life-forms and the appearance of man."[14]

According to the *Catechism*, God blesses the scientists involved in these discoveries:

> These discoveries invite us to even greater admiration for the greatness of the Creator, prompting us to give him thanks for all his works and for the understanding and wisdom he gives to scholars and researchers.[15]

In short, one might say that the church *quietly* accepts evolution as a scientific theory and sees no reason God the creator could not have used evolutionary processes in the emergence of the human species.[16]

However, the church still does not publicly acknowledge the tremendous impact this scientific information can have on our understanding of the purpose of human life in an evolutionary world.

Nevertheless, it is safe to say that the Catholic Church no longer prohibits the scientific study of evolution.

9. Does evolution threaten what the Bible teaches about creation?

Not really. The information modern science has provided simply gives a more accurate understanding of how the universe began and developed. The ancient biblical authors had no scientific method they could use to discover the age or size of the universe, so they told the creation story as best they could. Christians still believe that God created the universe. That is a truth that modern science can neither confirm nor deny.

10. Can the theory of evolution tell us how life on Earth originated?

The biological theory of evolution deals exclusively with observing how life has changed or evolved over time to produce the diversity of species we see today. It does not attempt to explain what originally caused life. Similarly, geology is concerned with studying how the rocks that make up Earth have changed over time, but it does not attempt to explain how Earth or any of the other stars and planets came to exist in the first place.

Biologists are not avoiding these questions. As a strict science, biology is not the field of study to answer these questions. No matter how life originated, the theory of evolution still remains the best explanation to account for the presence of so many living species on the planet. Questions about the origin of life are typically the domain of theologians, philosophers, and philosophers of science.

Historical Background

11. When did the conflict between the church and science begin?

The conflict between scientific evidence and biblical statements began most publicly in the seventeenth century. Until modern times, church leaders treated the Bible as a factually accurate document, even in its scientific and historical details. They reasoned that if God inspired the biblical writers, God would never allow them to write something that was inaccurate.

The church's conflict with science came to a head in the case of Galileo (1564–1642) and his telescope. Before then, the church and most people in the world believed that Earth was the fixed and unmoving center of the universe. Certainly, this belief about an unmoving Earth was held by scriptural authors at that time. Like the general public, these authors assumed that the sun and moon were orbs that circled Earth each day. After all, anyone could see that the sun rose in the east every morning and set in the west every evening. To this day, even scientists still refer to sunrise and sunset, speaking as if Earth is fixed and the sun orbits around it. However, what Galileo's telescope revealed was visible evidence that the opposite was true, namely, that Earth was a planet that orbited the sun. Galileo wrote a book describing the evidence.

The church banned his book in 1633 and threatened Galileo with excommunication, maybe even burning at the stake. This would be his expected punishment for making a claim that contradicted the Bible. Not wanting to lose his immortal soul, Galileo recanted. However, as he was leaving the Inquisition courtroom, it is rumored that he muttered regarding Earth, "But it's still moving."

More than a century passed before the Catholic Church declared in 1758 that it was not heretical to say that Earth revolved around the sun.[17] In 1822, the church lifted the ban on Galileo's book when it became common knowledge that Earth was not the center of the universe. As for Galileo himself, only in 1992 did the Vatican formally and publicly clear Galileo of any wrongdoing. More than three hundred years had passed before the church admitted that Galileo was right and cleared his name of heresy.

It is interesting to note that three years before the church's 1992 apology to Galileo, NASA had sent an exploratory spacecraft, named Galileo, to observe the planet Jupiter.

12. Why did the church fear modern science and evolution?

The publication of Charles Darwin's book *On the Origin of Species* in 1859 challenged statements about the description of the first human beings in the biblical book of Genesis. Church officials at the time insisted that the evidence of human evolution was *irreconcilable* with belief in the divine inspiration of scripture. Church officials in the nineteenth and early twentieth century insisted that the Bible was correct and accurate. It became a conflict about who was right, the Bible or the scientists.

The discovery of evolution called into question what the Bible said about the creation of the universe, its age and size, the origin of humanity as well as the origins of sin, evil, and death. Modern science discovered evidence of the origins of the universe and the origins of humanity that contradicted the biblical accounts. Thus, to accept evidence of evolution would seem to force the church to agree that many details in the Bible were not factual and accurate.

For example, in Genesis 1, the authors describe how God created the universe in six days. In their description, Earth was a flat disc and sat immovable at the center of the universe; each day the sun and moon orbited over and beneath it. The stars appeared to be countless little lights in a giant dome called the firmament. (Picture an enclosed giant sports stadium covered by a dome.) God's heavenly home was above the firmament. Genesis 2 states that God created the first two human beings as fully adult persons.

In contrast, scientists as early as the seventeenth century were asserting that Earth was merely one of several planets in space orbiting around the sun each year, that every star in the sky was a separate sun like our sun, probably with planets orbiting around it, that in our galaxy there were countless stars. Today, we know that our galaxy is but one of more than a hundred billion other galaxies in the known universe.

13. Why do some Christians believe the universe is only six thousand years old?

Some Christians believe that they can calculate how old the universe is by using genealogical evidence gleaned from the Bible. They trace the generations from Adam and Eve down to the birth of Jesus, accounting for about four thousand years. According to this biblical process, when you add the two thousand years of Christian history, the creation of the universe happened about six thousand years ago.

14. How old do scientists think the world is?

Scientists estimate the age of the universe at more than thirteen billion years old, and Earth at about four billion years old. Primitive cellular life appeared deep in Earth's oceans about one billion years ago. Earlier versions of the human species appeared in various places on Earth about one million years ago. *Homo sapiens* produced clear evidence of developed civilization about thirty thousand years ago.

There is no way that the minds of the biblical authors, or anyone else who lived three thousand years ago when the many books of the Bible were first being assembled into one, could even begin to grasp the kinds of scientific facts that we so easily absorb today. For example, could God have communicated to these ancient biblical scholars the fact that tectonic plates on which our continents rest can shift and, in colliding, can create mountains or produce earthquakes, undersea volcanoes, or tsunami tides? Could these men have grasped the idea that dinosaurs ruled Earth for over one hundred million years and disappeared from Earth about sixty-five million years ago? Or that Earth underwent ice ages periodically in its history?

15. Which popes were against evolution and modern science?

In the Catholic Church, formal resistance to the theory of evolution first began in the Catholic Church with Pope Leo XIII (papacy 1878–1903) and culminated in the encyclical of Pope Pius X (papacy 1903–14) called *Pascendi Dominici Gregis* (On the Doctrines of the Modernists) published in 1907.[18]

A few years later, in 1910, Pope Pius X issued a decree called The Oath against Modernism.[19] All priests and teachers in Catholic seminaries and universities were required to publicly recite this entire oath against promoting modern science and evolution. The oath, in effect, proved disheartening to Catholic scientists, especially anthropologists and geologists, like French Jesuit Pierre Teilhard de Chardin (1881–1955), who were discovering fossils of hominids that were evolutionary precursors of *Homo sapiens*.

Although the scientific community worldwide in general was bursting with scientific discoveries and advances during the twentieth century, the innovative work of Catholic scientists visibly diminished because of this oath. The teaching of evolution in Catholic schools and colleges was forbidden. The requirement of teachers to take this oath was in effect from 1910 until 1967, when Pope Paul VI (papacy 1963–78) finally rescinded it.

Evolution in the United States

16. How did Christians in the United States react to evolution?

As evolution came to be accepted as a scientific principle in biology, many southern states in the so-called Bible Belt passed laws against teaching evolution in public school classrooms. Perhaps the clearest example of the conflict between evolution and the Bible was played out in the famous so-called Scopes Monkey Trial.

The trial was held in Dayton, Tennessee, and began on July 10, 1925. John Thomas Scopes, a young high school science teacher, was accused of teaching evolution in violation of a Tennessee statute called the Butler Act. This law had been passed by the legislature and signed by the governor a few months before, in March. The Butler Act made it a misdemeanor punishable by fine to "teach any theory that denies the story of the Divine Creation of man as taught in the Bible, and to teach instead that man has descended from a lower order of animals."

With the help of a local businessman, Tom Scopes conspired to get himself charged with a violation of the Butler Act, in order to challenge it. After his arrest, Scopes and the businessman enlisted the aid of the American Civil Liberties Union (ACLU) to organize a defense.

Hearing of this coordinated attack on Christian fundamentalism, William Jennings Bryan, a three-time Democratic presidential candidate and a biblical fundamentalist hero, volunteered to assist the prosecution. Once Bryan agreed to present the prosecution's side, the famous trial attorney Clarence Darrow decided to join the ACLU on the defense's side. Thus, the stage was set for one of the most famous trials in U.S. history.

Soon after the announcement of the trial, hordes of spectators and news reporters descended on Dayton, Tennessee. The town took on a carnival-like atmosphere. On sidewalks near the courthouse, vendors sold Bibles, toy monkeys, hot dogs, and lemonade. An exhibit opened featuring live chimpanzees. A short man with a protruding jaw masqueraded around the courthouse as a chimp dressed in a plaid suit, a brown fedora, and white spats. Not to be left out, local preachers set up revival tents along the city's main street to keep the Bible-faithful stirred up. Local and national newspapers and magazines sent reporters and photographers to cover the spectacle.

Inside the courthouse, Darrow first tried, unsuccessfully, to convince the judge that the law was unconstitutional. The Christian judge also refused Darrow's request to stop opening each day's proceeding with prayer.

The following day, fearing that the weight of the crowd inside would collapse the courtroom floor, the judge ordered the trial moved outdoors to the courthouse lawn. The trial continued in the open air in front of several thousand spectators. It was a warm July in Tennessee.

In a surprise tactical twist by the defense, the only witness Darrow called was the prosecution's lawyer, Bryan himself. Under Darrow's questioning, Bryan was subjected to severe ridicule and forced to make contradictory statements, to the amusement of the crowd. The press recorded the verbal exchange for their papers. The court battle went on for ten days.

On July 21, in his closing speech, Darrow simply asked the jury to return a verdict of guilty in order that the case might be appealed. The judge accepted the request and sent the jury inside to deliberate. After only eight minutes, the jury returned with a guilty verdict, and the judge ordered Tom Scopes to pay a fine of one hundred dollars, the minimum the law allowed. The case was over.

Although Bryan had won the case by Darrow conceding his client's guilt, Bryan had been publicly humiliated. Even more frustrating, he was thereby denied the opportunity to deliver the closing speech he had been preparing for weeks.

Details of Darrow's examination of Bryan during the trial appeared in newspapers and magazines nationwide, challenging his fundamentalist beliefs. From then on, the conflict between science and the Bible became a wedge splitting in two the people of the United States.

17. What were some of the attitudes toward teaching evolution in American public schools after the Scopes Monkey trial?

The Scopes trial had both short- and long-term effects in the teaching of science in public schools in the United States. The trial clearly revealed a growing split in American Christianity since most Americans at the time belonged to a Christian denomination.

During the first half of the twentieth century, the majority of Christians denounced evolution. The Scopes trial simply escalated the political and legal conflict between strict creationists and scientists. Scientists insisted on teaching natural evolution. Creationists believed the Bible was the authoritative document, thereby trumping scientific claims. Some proposed that there were two ways of finding truth, one "biblical" and one "evolutionist."

After Scopes was convicted, creationists throughout the United States sought to pass similar anti-evolution laws for their states. The Butler Act that had convicted Scopes survived in Tennessee until 1967. After the Scopes trial, Mississippi and Arkansas put anti-evolution laws, which lasted into the 1970s, on their books.

The Scopes trial also had its effects on high school biology texts in the 1930s and 1940s. Among the most widely used textbooks after the trial, only one included the word *evolution* in its index; moreover, the relevant page included biblical quotations.

18. When did American attitudes toward evolution begin to change?

In 1958, shortly after Russia had launched *Sputnik* in the fall of 1957, the National Defense Educational Act was passed. Many legislators feared the United States education system was falling behind that of the Soviet Union. Subsequently, textbooks, produced in cooperation with the American Institute of Biological Sciences, stressed the importance of evolution as the unifying principle of biology.

A strong backlash to the new textbooks began in Texas. Attacks were launched in sermons and in the press. Complaints were lodged with the State Textbook Commission. However, the resistance was weakened for two reasons. In addition to federal support of science and the successes of American science, a number of social trends had turned public discussion in favor of evolution, such as an increased interest in improving public education, legal precedents separating religion and public education, and continued urbanization in the South.

During the 1960s, the opponents of natural evolution transitioned from the anti-evolution crusade of the 1920s to the "creation science" movement. Creation scientists shifted from overtly religious to covertly religious objections to evolutionary theory. They claimed to have developed scientific evidence in support of a literal interpretation of the Bible.

19. What is "creation science"?

Creation science takes many forms, all of which differ from a "theistic evolution" position. Theistic evolution accepts science's evidence that we live in an evolving world, and it allows that God, from the beginning, probably intended to create an evolving world. In contrast, all forms of "creation science" reject both modern science's methods and its natural evolutionary explanations. In its place, creation scientists affirm the biblical explanation.

In general, forms of creation science assert that creation stories in the Book of Genesis were *factual truth*. Creation science founders claimed that their positions were "scientific" and therefore qualified for inclusion in science textbooks in American public schools. They claimed that creation science should be taught as an alternative to the strictly natural evolutionary views of modern science.

20. What is "creationism"?

Pure "creationism" is among the most strictly Bible-based forms of creation science. In general, creationism proposes that the universe and each species of its living organisms (fish, plants, trees, animals, and so on) originated from specific acts of the divine Creator. Creationism teaches that biblical accounts of the events in the creation of the universe happened exactly as they were described in the first three chapters of Genesis, and not by any natural processes such as evolution. In other words, creationism claims that the universe and each of the life forms that we see on Earth today *as they exist today* were created in the six days of creation by God. All species—cows, sheep, horses, elephants, wolves, camels, mice, mosquitoes, gerbils, otters, snakes, and aardvarks—were put on Earth specifically and individually by divine action at the beginning. In other words, creationism accepts the biblical account of creation as scientifically correct.

21. Are there other forms of creation science?

Yes, quite a few. More recent forms of creation science have come to accept a more realistic approach to geological time. Others began to support what they called a more "progressive creationism" or "neo-creationism." However, all forms of creationism or creation science continue to reject natural evolutionary explanations—or at a minimum they would like their biblical creation science theories to appear in science textbooks as an alternate *scientific* explanation of the universe.

However, a series of court decisions ruled out the teaching of creationism or creation science in American public schools, stating that its principles were more appropriate for courses in philosophy or theology, rather than in a science class.[20]

22. What is "intelligent design"?

The intelligent design approach was originally planned as a rebranding of creation science to avoid a series of court decisions that had eliminated creationism as a science. Intelligent design asserts that "certain features of the universe and of living things are best explained by an intelligent cause, not an undirected [evolutionary] process such as natural selection." The aim of this group of creation science theorists was to replace the secular scientific method with "a science consonant with Christian and theistic convictions" that accepts and integrates certain supernatural explanations. In the courts, however, intelligent design suffered the same fate as other forms of creation science.

In the United States, teaching of "intelligent design" in public schools has been decisively ruled by a federal district court to be in violation of the First Amendment to the United States Constitution. The court found that intelligent design does not qualify as science and "cannot uncouple itself from its creationist, and thus religious, antecedents," and hence cannot be taught as an alternative to evolution in public school science classrooms under the jurisdiction of that court.[21]

23. How has the fear of evolution affected Catholics in science?

Despite the opinions of the courts, Christian fundamentalists continue to reject natural evolution, either explicitly or implicitly. Some publicly try to deny or ridicule evolution, while others simply refuse to talk about it. Meanwhile, many scientific advances continue to be made clarifying evolutionary geological discoveries regarding our human ancestry.

These discoveries get little to no mention from the pulpit. The word *evolution* remains taboo in many American churches and in religious households. Even churches that accept theistic evolution maintain silence about scientific evolution.

From another vantage point, the Christian fear of modern science and specifically evolution has affected the Catholic Church's contributions to science in the last half of the twentieth century. One study compared the number of Nobel Prizes won by scientists who professed to be Catholic Christians with those who professed to be atheists, agnostics, nonbelievers, or having no church affiliation. Here are the simple totals for Nobel Prize winners from 1950 through 2010 in scientific fields:

Nobel Prize Winners (1950–2010)[22]		
	Atheists/Nonbelievers	Catholics
Physics	30	1
Chemistry	14	2
Medicine	19	1
Economics	7	3
TOTAL	70	7

Thus, the final score for Nobel Prize winners in the three scientific areas is: atheists 70, Catholics 7.

Despite the poor showing of Catholics, the human species as a whole has clearly been growing and evolving.

On the other hand, many of the advances made in science and mathematics in the last twenty centuries were made by Christians. Deserving special notice are the contributions of bishops, priests, monks, and members of religious orders.[23] With such a radical change witnessed in the comparison of Nobel Prize winners from 1950 to 2010, it is difficult not to place some of the blame on the church's mistrust of modern science and evolution for this dramatic downturn.

24. What do some mainline Protestant churches currently say about evolution?[24]

As early as 1982, the *Episcopal Church* passed a resolution to "affirm its belief in the glorious ability of God to create in any manner." In their *Catechism of Creation*, Episcopalians also rejected "the rigid dogmatism of the 'Creationist' movement" and expressed skepticism toward the "intelligent design" movement.[25]

As of 2014, the *Evangelical Lutheran Church in America* had not issued a definitive statement on evolution. It did affirm that "God created the universe and all that is therein, only not necessarily in six 24-hour days, and that God actually may have used evolution in the process of creation."[26]

In contrast, the *Lutheran Church–Missouri Synod* teaches that "the Genesis account of Creation is true and factual, not merely a 'myth' or 'story' made up to explain the origin of all things." This branch of the Lutheran Church rejects evolution or any theory that "denies or limits the work of creation as taught in Scripture."[27]

In 1969, the *Presbyterian Church*'s governing body affirmed that evolution and the Bible do not contradict each other.[28] Still, this church body has stated that, officially, it "should carefully refrain from either affirming or denying the theory of evolution." Its church doctrine continues to hold that human beings are a unique creation of God, "made in His own image."[29]

In 2008, the *United Methodist Church*'s highest legislative body passed a resolution saying, "science's descriptions of cosmological, geological, and biological evolution are not in conflict with [the church's] theology." Moreover, the document added "many apparent scientific references in [the] Bible...are intended to be metaphorical [and] were included to help understand the religious principles, but not to teach science."[30]

The *United Church of Christ* finds evolutionary theory and Christian faith to be compatible, embracing evolution as a means "to see our faith in a new way."[31]

In 1982, the *Southern Baptist Convention* issued a resolution rejecting the theory of evolution, suggesting a clear separation between church and science. If science is proposing theories about creation they are to be "presented solely in terms of scientific evidence without any religious doctrines or concepts." Some Southern Baptist leaders have spoken out in favor of creationism and the intelligent design movement.[32]

25. Is there a way to reconcile the claims of science and religion? How?

Yes. There is a clear way to distinguish the books of the Bible from textbooks in physics, chemistry, biology, and the other sciences.

Experts in each field are writing in very different domains and from very different perspectives. The domains of science and religion are not in conflict but are complementary.

The Bible is a book recounting the story of God's relationship to humanity. It is focused on moral and theological truths, not on the factual accuracy of its history or technical details regarding the appearance of millions of different life forms. Sacred texts write about moral and spiritual events, good and evil. Genesis 1 asserts theological truths, for example, that God created the universe, and that humanity is responsible for caring for Earth and the creatures on it.

In contrast, science operates solely in the physical domain. It is concerned with accumulating measurable facts as well as formulas to explain these facts. The materials of its research are things happening in space and time. According to its scientific principles, science cannot affirm or deny anything about God, or the existence or nonexistence of God because God is not a physical, measurable entity.

Christians need to agree that the ancient biblical authors cannot be held responsible for lacking the accuracy of modern scientific tools to calculate immense time periods or to understand the intricate workings of the physical universe. Believers, in turn, need to respect and admire the wonderful accomplishments of science in helping us understand the workings of the physical universe.

Scientists need to agree that science cannot deny or reject religious, moral, and spiritual values simply because these factors cannot be identified or measured with scientific instruments. Scientists can respect what religions bring to daily life and civilization, namely, the dimension of morality and ethics, such as respect for life and freedom for all, the protection of the underprivileged, and care for the life of our planet. These factors are important in governing the use of scientific advancements such as nuclear weapons and chemical and biological warfare.

26. What are some lessons to learn?

Because people of faith accept responsibility for caring for the earth and its creatures, they should want to become scientists and technicians and excel in their work and research *precisely because they believe in God*.

In turn, scientists and technicians are challenged to use scientific facts and formulas to create tools for the enrichment and the future of human life.

The Creation Story according to Scripture and Science

27. What is the central message in the biblical account of the creation story?

The Nicene Creed states it very simply: *"I believe in one God, the Father almighty, maker of heaven and earth, of all things visible and invisible."* This is the core of Christian beliefs about creation.

More important for us today in our climate crisis, the creed and Genesis 1:9–31 confirms creation's ecological unity, that is, that the universe is one inextricably connected reality. With this statement about Earth being a single immense organism science totally agrees. Human beings cannot survive without nature. Without nature, there would be no air to breathe, no water to sustain life, no food to eat, no sun to warm and give light. Our brains and nervous system need the nourishment of minerals and metals in order to function. For the believer, the creedal statement and these biblical verses are a clear expression of the wonderful unity between creation and Creator.

28. Does evolution threaten what the Bible teaches about humanity's origins?

Not really. The information modern science has provided simply gives a more accurate understanding of how long ago the universe began and how it developed. The ancient biblical authors had no scientific method they could use to discover the age or size of the universe, so they told the creation story as best they could. Christians and people of other faith traditions still believe that God created the universe. That is a truth that modern science can neither confirm nor deny.

Modern geology and anthropology assure us that the origin of humanity did not happen as the Adam and Eve story tells it in Genesis 2 and 3. However, the important truths in those chapters about the fallible nature of the human person and humanity's responsibility to care for and protect Earth remain true and irrefutable.

29. If modern science has shown that the story of creation in the Bible is incorrect regarding the age of the universe and the origins of humanity, does this mean that the Bible cannot be trusted?

The Bible was never meant to be a scientifically and historically accurate document. It is primarily a document about God's relation to humanity. The biblical authors had no intention of writing a science textbook. They were Jews preserving in words the story of their people's understanding of God and their relationship with the Creator.

From our perspective in the twenty-first century, there is no way that these authors over three thousand years ago could have grasped the idea of creation happening as a cosmic singularity of countless subatomic particles bursting forth from a single "Big Bang." They could never have grasped the fact that their sun was in fact just one among the billions of stars in our galaxy. They would never have believed that Earth was a planet in orbit around the sun; their common sense told them it was the Earth that was fixed and the sun that rotated around it each day. They would have understood nothing about the origins of cellular life, its genetic makeup, or the universal sharing of DNA. They would have laughed if you suggested that their human body and brain was the outcome of many millions of years of evolutionary development.

If all this is true, then clearly it would be in vain to expect that God could have communicated to these ancient writers current information from astronomy, biology, genetics, geology, and anthropology, so that their religious texts would be scientifically accurate.

Although the Bible does not present scientifically and historically accurate facts, it can give us wisdom, guidance, understanding, purpose, and meaning in life. It can help us discern how God would like us to live our lives on Earth and cooperate with what God is doing in the world.

30. If creation stories are not historical documents, what is their purpose?

Almost all cultures have their own creation stories—legends handed down from generation to generation. These stories were typically shaped and shared by the spiritual leaders or the priestly class in each nation and were intended to provide answers to the most fundamental existential questions that human beings asked. Such questions might take the form: How was Earth created? How did it come to be the way it is? Are there supernatural powers? What do they want from us? How do we know what is right and wrong? Why is giving birth so painful? Why is physical work so hard? Why is there evil in the world? Why is there suffering and death?

Community leaders developed creation stories to answer such questions. These spiritual leaders were not scientists, as we use the term today. Their sacred stories may not have been true in today's scientific sense, but they contained important truths for living and shaping their community's life.

Today, to find out the truth—or the facts—of how the universe came to be, we turn, not to the priestly class or the artists, but to scientists. Using their scientific instruments, they have been able to trace back in time with much more accuracy to the first few moments after the Big Bang—the moment of creation. Much of the information they have gleaned from over a hundred years of study requires us to call into question the factualness of the scriptural accounts of creation.

However, using its scientific instruments alone, science can say nothing explicitly to us about God or the purpose and meaning of creation, since that is not the domain or expertise of science; it is the domain of philosophers, theologians, and religious leaders. Integration of this scientific information into theological thinking is a major challenge facing religions today.

Until a few centuries ago, almost no one but a handful of astronomers challenged the accuracy of the biblical creation stories. In the seventeenth century, the primary theological difficulty was to integrate the fact that Earth revolved around the sun, and not vice versa, as was the traditional belief. Until that time, Earth was considered to be the center of the universe and the total focus of God's concern.

In the seventeenth and eighteenth centuries, little else about the biblical creation stories, such as Adam and Eve and the Garden of Eden, received much scientific challenge. However, more recent scientific discoveries in physics, astronomy, biology, chemistry, anthropology, and geology have begun to call into question many of the "facts" presented in the early chapters of the Hebrew Scriptures.

Nevertheless, contemporary facts and information about the origin and development of our universe, as well as the evolution of life forms on Earth, all need to be reinterpreted again by theologians to give this new data purpose and meaning for humanity. Jesuit priest Pierre Teilhard de Chardin was one of the first theologian-scientists to attempt such integration, but he never developed a new creation myth for our time as powerful and colorful as the ones we find in Genesis.

31. What are the sources of the creation stories in the Hebrew Scriptures?

First, it is important to recognize that Genesis contains two distinctly different stories of creation. Chapter 1 contains one complete creation story, how the universe was made in six days. Chapters 2—4 contain a second creation story, about Adam and Eve and the Garden of Eden.

The Hebrew Scriptures were developed and assembled by Jewish scholars around five hundred years before Christ. Biblical experts identify four different groups that contributed to the development and assembly of the Bible. The four groups were: (1) the *Elohists*, who always called God by the generic name for God, *Elohim*; (2) the *Yahwists*, who most often called God by the specific name *Yahweh*; (3) the *Priestly Group*, who represented the interests of the temple and worship; and (4) the *Deuteronomists*, who were the lawyers and scribes who defined rules of social behavior as well as laws related to food, cleanliness, property, legal issues, and the like.

If you use a Bible with scholarly footnotes, the notes will tell you which of the four groups was responsible for a particular chapter or parts of a chapter. Elohists are often referred to simply by the letter *E*, Yahwists by the letter *J*,[33] Priests by the letter *P*, and Deuteronomists by the letter *D*.

The first creation story came from the Elohists. In Genesis 1, *Elohim* is a "distant" God, a transcendent creator. *Elohim* created humanity but never directly interacted with any human beings. *Elohim* simply assigned to humanity responsibility ("dominion") over Earth and all the creatures on it.

The second creation story found in chapters 2—4 came from the Yahwist tradition. Yahweh is very different from the "distant" *Elohim*. Yahweh is personally involved with Adam. Yahweh and Adam have frequent conversations. Yahweh brings animals to Adam for him to name. Yahweh accompanies Adam for walks in the garden. Yahweh taught him how to till the soil. Yahweh makes a female helpmate for Adam. Yahweh gives Adam and Eve instructions about life and a commandment not to eat the fruit of a certain tree in the center of the garden.

32. What does the story of Adam and Eve and the Garden of Eden teach us?

The Yahwist (*J*) writers of Genesis 2, 3, and 4 provide the origins and explanations of more than twenty basic teachings upon which the Hebrew religion, societal structure, and culture were based: the creation of the soul, the primacy of the male, the subordination of the female, the structure of marriage, the seriousness of

God's commandments, the definition of sin and its consequences, the sources of temptation to sin, the reason why work is so hard, why childbearing is so painful, and that death is inevitable. Please remember that the story, especially in its description of the social roles and moral quality of women, reflects Hebrew thinking half a millennium before Christ.

Here is a partial list of the elements of the story and what they were intended to teach:

- First, a male is formed from "dust of the earth." (*The human body is made from elements of the earth; primacy of the male, Gen 2:7.*)
- God breathes into the male "the breath of life." (*God creates the soul, Gen 2:7.*)
- God "planted a garden" for the man. (*God provides ways to produce food, Gen 2:8.*)
- God plants the "tree of life" and the "tree of the knowledge of good and evil." (*Original innocence of humans, Gen 2:9*)
- God provides water for humans. (*Gen 2:10–14*)
- God assigns man the role "to till the garden and keep it." (*Origins of agriculture, Gen 2:15*)
- "Of the tree of the knowledge of good and evil you shall not eat." (*God gives first commandment and states the consequence of disobedience, Gen 2:16.*)
- Death is the result of disobedience of God's commandments. (*Hebrew explanation of how human death came to be, Gen 2:17*)
- God provides animals and birds to relieve the man's loneliness. (*Gen 2:18*)
- God gives man the right to "name" all other creatures. (*The male is the one who decides what to name each creature and child, Gen 2:19; also, animals were made from the earth as the man was.*)

- Animals are unsatisfactory as helpers or equal partners of the man. (*Gen 2:20*)
- Woman is made from man's rib, not from the earth. (*Subordination of woman to man, woman as property of and part of the man, Gen 2:22*)
- The man exercises his right to be the name-giver and names "woman." (*Gen 2:23*)
- Man and woman joined together are "one flesh." (*Definition of marriage; the union of the two persons generates a new being, that is, "one flesh," Gen 2:24*)
- Human beings who are innocent of sin are not ashamed of the human body. (*The origin of shame comes from human sin, Gen 2:25. Also, acknowledgement of human self-reflective consciousness and self-conviction, for example, knowing what you are doing and knowing that what you are doing is right or wrong.*)
- "Serpent" symbolizes worldly temptations. (*Note that there are no other human beings yet and no devils, so the authors make the serpent, a crafty wild creature, the tempter. Temptations come from the world around us, Gen 3:1.*)
- The fruit on the tree appears to be good food, a delight to the eyes, and will make one wise. (*Temptations usually come in the form of "good" or the appearance of good, Gen 3:6.*)
- Woman is the first to sin. (*Woman is the source of sin and leads man to sin, Gen 3:6.*)
- Man blames woman for his eating the forbidden fruit. (*Blaming and scapegoating begin, Gen 3:12.*)
- Woman blames the "serpent." (*Tempter is the source of evil; devil is a trickster, Gen 3:13.*)
- "They knew that they were naked"; they covered their nakedness. (*One consequence of sin is shame; also establishes the social need to wear clothing, Gen 3:7.*)

- Disobedient man and woman attempt to hide from God but are unsuccessful. (*God sees and knows all things, Gen 3:8.*)
- In punishment for tempting human beings, God brings a "curse" upon the serpent. (*Great fear of snakes among the Hebrews? Gen 3:14*)
- The curse does not apply to animals. (*Animals remain innocent; they are not disobedient to God, Gen 3:14.*)
- Disobedience brings the pains of childbirth to the woman. (*Gen 3:16*)
- "And he shall rule over you." (*God assigns the woman to obey the man, Gen 3:16.*)
- God curses the ground because of man's disobedience, and the man gets the punishment of toil as he farms the earth. (*The pain of toil and sweat; Earth's resistance to man's efforts; food is no longer free as it was in the garden; man must grow his own food; need to sweat and toil is the result of sin, Gen 3:17–18.*)
- "You are dust and to dust you shall return." (*Sentence of death; because of sin, death would come to each one in due course, Gen 3:19.*)
- Humans now understand the difference between good and evil. (*Gen 3:22*)
- Humans are driven from the Garden lest "they eat of the tree of life and live forever." (*Humans are finite and must die, Gen 3:22, 24.*)
- Jealousy, envy, anger, hatred, deception, and murder. (*Variety of sins introduced, Gen 4*)

Although some of these teachings (such as male superiority over females) simply reflect the male-dominant culture of the ancient world, many teachings remain good ethical and moral principles.

33. The Bible states that suffering and death began with the sin of our first parents. Is this true?

Science assures us that suffering and death did not begin with the first human beings, as the Bible suggests. Suffering and death were a natural part of existence long before the first human beings appeared on planet Earth. Plants died, fish died, insects died, animals suffered and died. And as we now know, even stars like our sun died or were swallowed into black holes in outer space. All of this happened eons before the first human beings appeared on Earth. Much suffering in the natural world is unavoidable.

What humanity brought into the world was *avoidable* suffering and *avoidable* death, produced by war, deprivation, weaponry, slavery, unfairness, manipulation of wealth and resources, punishment, abuse, and a host of other evils.

PART 2

HOW EVOLUTION WORKS

Let's talk about how God keeps creation both good and new—which means always going somewhere even better. I know some Christians might be hesitant about this, but the helpful word here is "evolution." God keeps creating things from the inside out, so they are forever yearning, developing, growing, and changing for the good.

Richard Rohr[1]

Some Basics of Evolution

34. How should you approach studying evolution?

Evolution is not a mystery. It is not scary. It does not threaten your faith. It is not unusual. It is quite common and familiar to everyone. Think of studying evolution as a learning experience. Think of it as exploring a new aspect of God that you never thought about before now. After all, if God created the universe, and the universe is evolving, then God must have created an *evolving* universe. Think of this section as learning a bit about how God managed this evolutionary creating.

35. When did scientists first become aware of evolution?

The scientific exploration of the phenomenon of evolution was shared with the world by the publication of Charles Darwin's *On the Origin of Species* in 1859. Darwin provided a book full of clear evidence that an evolutionary process is at work everywhere among biological creatures. For example, he showed that new species of birds and flowers were happening naturally. Darwin's drawings captured images of four distinct species of finches that had evolved from a parent group. He postulated that changes occurred over several generations as the birds gradually adapted to various changing environments, weather conditions, and availability of food. He called the evolutionary process "adaptation to environment."

36. How do biologists understand and define *biological evolution* today?

Biology became the primary scientific field that studied evolution and the processes that produced it. As biologists learned more about how genetic inheritance worked, their understanding of the evolutionary process went beyond the simple "adaptation to environment" process of Darwin. Textbooks on biology began to provide entire chapters on the evolutionary process. Then, entire books on evolution.

Biology's definition of *biological evolution* has itself evolved. Definitions became quite technical, sophisticated, and very precise. Sadly, biologists often defined *evolution* scientifically in terms unknown to the ordinary educated reader. Fortunately, a few biologists provided some definitions accessible to the rest of us.

Here is a common short definition of *evolution* that can be found in many textbooks: "Evolution can be precisely defined as any change in the frequency of alleles within a gene pool from one generation to the next."[2] These alleles are found in a creature's DNA.

A DNA molecule is like a long string made up of a certain *sequence* of elements. You may picture DNA like a yearly calendar that is made up of a fixed sequence of elements. January is followed by February, followed by March, and so on, is a fixed sequence. Similarly, the days of the week follow a certain sequence: Sunday is always followed by Monday, Monday is always followed by Tuesday. An allele describes a variation in the sequence. Suppose we were to have May and September switch places every year from now on. That would be an "allele" in the calendar. Similarly, if we were to have days of the week change their sequence, say, Friday switches places with Monday every month from now on, that would be another "allele" in the calendar. Biological evolution happens when one or more fixed sequences of elements are similarly changed or switched within a species gene pool. Unfortunately, such a definition of evolution using alleles is accessible and identifiable only using an electron microscope.

Another more general definition of evolution, a bit easier to grasp because it uses visible evidence, is "Evolution is a process that results in heritable changes in a population spread over many generations."

Heritable is a very general term. It has two basic meanings. It refers to any trait or ability that is either (1) genetic or inheritable, or (2) acquired or learned. The first produces new abilities through *nature*; the second produces new abilities through *nurture*. These new abilities can be passed from parents to their children:

1. Genetic traits are directly passed down from parents to children, by nature, in their genetic makeup. We have no control over these. Genetic traits include eye color, hair color, skin color, right- or left-handedness, bone structure, height, blood type, intelligence, and certain illnesses like schizophrenia and sickle-cell anemia. Many things that happen to parents are not automatically passed on to children, such as physical deformities, most chronic diseases, mental illnesses, birthmarks, and tattoos.
2. Acquired or nurtured traits may be learned and passed on through

    - *observation* (watching how others behave and use language)
    - *practice* (as in developing facility in any skill such as sports or music)
    - *education* (mental skills acquired through books, media, schooling)
    - *social customs* (popular clothing styles, manners, food preferences)

For biologists, the evolutionary process of natural selection operates only through genetic makeup, that is, by *nature*. They do not acknowledge the evolution of acquired traits, despite the fact that such acquired traits may prove to produce evolutionary effects in other areas. For example, thirty thousand years ago, humanity had not developed written languages or mathematics, yet today much of the world knows how to read and write and use numbers. Such basic skills became highly developed so that today human beings are able to fly to the moon and Mars. Quite an evolutionary step for humanity!

37. According to biologists, can an acquired trait evolve?

Biologists answer no. By their definition of evolution, they say that *individuals do not evolve, only populations evolve*. In other words, biologists refuse to make evolutionary statements about individuals. Only when a new trait appears consistently in many individuals within a population of plants or animals do biologists observe or recognize an evolutionary event. Typically, plant and animal evolution happens biologically when a group of certain animals or birds separate themselves and migrate to a different environment and undergo a series of natural selections until a new trait emerges.

When biologists say that humans and chimps have evolved from a common ancestor, they mean that there have been successive genetic changes in the two separated populations since they separated.

Biological evolution requires a change in the properties of populations of organisms, properties that transcend the lifetime of any single individual. Changes in populations that are considered evolutionary are those that are inheritable via genetic material passed down from one generation to the next.

Biological evolution may be slight or substantial; it embraces everything from slight changes in the proportion of different alleles (sequences) within a population (such as those determining blood types) to the successive alterations that led from the earliest protoorganism to amazing differences in snails, bees, giraffes, and dandelions.

38. Is biological evolution the only kind of evolution there is?

Not at all. If the biological definition of *evolution* provided the only kind of evolution, there would be nothing more to say. However, a respected evolutionary biologist preferred a more inclusive definition. He defined *evolution* in its broadest sense, as all-pervasive. According to this more general definition, evolution may be found *wherever there is significant change in the abilities of a "species."*

We could include in the term *species* things as different as galaxies, languages, or political systems. In this extended sense, evolution is all-pervasive.

In this book, we accept this broad definition of *evolution*. In this way, we can learn to look for and identify evolution happening at every level of existence and in every level of human life.

Thus, biologists are not the only people who need to study evolution. They're not the only ones who know about it and have to deal with it. Evolution is a familiar experience to all of us. We probably did not recognize some special trait or ability as an evolutionary event when it happened. We might have described it as growing, developing, maturing, improving. Once you grasp evolution's simple definition, you will realize that you are quite familiar with evolution. It is happening all around you, and *to* you.

39. What is a simple definition of *evolution*?

When something appears in a "species" that is genuinely new and different from who or what was before, we can say that this "species" has evolved. That's a simple definition that describes the process of evolution.

It is important to note the words *genuinely different*. In this definition, *species* is understood in the widest sense. For example, there are various "species" of mathematics, such as algebra, geometry, calculus, probability, set theory, and number theory. Evolution may occur in any of these species. There are "species" of communication, such as personal letters, emails, newspapers, magazines, journals, radio, television, and phones. Evolution may occur in each of these species.

40. Is evolution different from change or improvement?

Although evolution requires change, every change is not an evolutionary event. For example, we can change the *name* of a product, an animal, or a plant. The new name does not mean that the product or creature has evolved. We can change the color of a product or its label. We can strengthen the formula of a product, say, of a certain laundry soap, so that its performance is improved, and it may make clothes whiter or fluffier than other products. These are merely differences in degree. But until we can show that this improvement has generated properties or abilities beyond other laundry soaps, we cannot claim that it has evolved. New traits, properties, or abilities are the clearest signs of evolution.

41. Is evolution different from revolution?

Yes. In *revolution*, the species, thing, or situation that existed before is destroyed, overthrown, or done away with. For example, politically, before 1917, Russia was a monarchy ruled by the Tsars. Their rule was overthrown by a people's revolution in 1917. Government by a single ruler was done away with and replaced by communism.

A couple of centuries earlier in North America, a revolution overthrew colonial rule by a British king. It was replaced it by a democratic government that became the United States. In each case, the old political order was replaced by a new political order. Revolutions typically destroy what they replace.

In contrast, *in evolution nothing is destroyed*. Evolution is characterized by advancement or enrichment of what went before without destroying what went before. Many new species of plants, fish, birds, and animals have evolved, yet the earlier species from which they evolved still continue to exist. In technology, the smart phone has evolved from the landline phone and the mobile phone, yet many homes still use a landline phone or a mobile phone. In the animal world, dogs evolved from the gray wolf, but gray wolves still exist as their own species.

Typically, something that has evolved has come from something that went before it. We might say that each newly evolved thing had "parents." For example, at one point early in the twentieth century, the phenomenon of television appeared. It possessed new and different properties, but it didn't appear out of nowhere. It had "parents," namely, radio and film. These two technologies were mated and produced their evolved offspring, television.

In the natural world, fruit growers mated an orange and a tangerine to produce a new and different fruit, the tangelo, which has the juiciness of an orange and the easily peelable skin of a tangerine.

42. What is a clear sign of evolution?

We can usually say that *something has evolved if it has "emergent properties,"* that is, *it possesses qualities, abilities, or capacities that neither of its "parents" alone had.* For example, television can do things that neither radio nor film can do alone. Radio itself is incapable of showing pictures, and traditional film in a theater cannot be broadcast simultaneously into ten million homes at once. Thus, television qualifies as an evolved medium because of its emergent properties.

The word-processor software on a computer has many editorial emergent properties beyond those of a typewriter. A word processor can correct misspellings; cut-and-paste words, sentences, and paragraphs; change typeface or type size in a moment; change print to italics or boldface instantly, and so on. A computer is an evolved instrument for writing. Because most of the people on the planet use computers, we can say that it marks an evolutionary step in *Homo sapiens*'s life.

Shopping is another simple example of evolution happening to humanity. Easy shopping for anything from food to furniture to medicines to books and thousands of other things is a process that has evolved. In humanity's early days, if you wanted food, you hunted for it. If you wanted clothing, you made it yourself. If you wanted to "buy" something from another person, you traded something you owned or made yourself. The invention of money was a great evolutionary step in shopping. You no longer had to trade or barter. You could buy it with money.

A century ago, if you wanted to buy something, you had to physically walk to a grocery store or take a bus "downtown" to a department store to buy it. Today, we can buy things using *online transactions*. Without leaving the comfort of your living room sofa, you can use your computer or smart phone to buy almost anything from anywhere in the world and have it delivered to your door. You can still shop at a grocery store or a shop at the mall. But online shopping qualifies as an evolution in shopping.

How Evolution Happens

43. In what ways can *evolution* happen?

Evolution can occur in at least three ways: (1) gradually, through a series of small mutations, in a process called *natural selection*; (2) by way of *symbiosis*, the joining or mating of two different sources to produce an evolved offspring; or (3) in a *combination* of both processes.

Natural Selection. Evolution can come about when some members of a species leave their natural environment and in a new environment undergo a series of mutations or slight changes over time. In this case, after a number of generations, the most recent offspring develop emergent properties that the original species did not have, thus qualifying as "evolved."

For example, Charles Darwin, the father of evolutionary theory, studied a species of birds with strong short beaks that lived on the mainland. Some of these birds flew to a distant island to establish nests there. However, the best source of food on the island could be found only in flower nectar. Over generations, the species "naturally selected" for mating those birds with the longest, narrowest beaks. Eventually, when Darwin returned some years later, he discovered that the original migrated birds, over time, had become a new species; they had become expert at reaching deep into flower blossoms to extract the nectar. The long narrow beak of these birds was an "emergent property" that none of the mainland birds possessed.

We human beings consciously use education and training in much the same ways on ourselves. We evolve as persons and communities by developing new abilities and capacities. Groups of people study an area of learning and over time, little by little, develop a proficiency that was not present in them when they began their education.

Improved and/or new study methods are another way of helping individuals or groups to evolve. This is evolution gradually through a *series of small steps or mutations*.

For example, if you took an ordinary person off the street and handed the person a violin and a bow, that person couldn't make music with the violin. But, with training by a good teacher, over time, the person, with sufficient practice, could develop the unique capacity to play a violin. Once enough people are trained as musicians to perform, and others are trained to compose music, a culture can develop and multiply jazz combos, community bands, and symphony orchestras.

Similarly, you can randomly select a person and ask them to peer into an electron microscope and describe what they see. Most will say that they see a scene filled with little squirming things. The normal person can make little sense of what is seen, but expert biologists, who evolved gradually in the art of deciphering and identifying various molecules, can easily identify the various microscopic objects on the slide. This new equipment, the electron microscope, enabled *the entire field of biology to evolve* through a *series of small steps*.

Similarly, the artistic fields of painting, sculpting, and architecture have evolved step-by-step. So have the culinary arts. So have political systems and so on. There seems to be new evolutionary potential everywhere you look.

44. Can individuals evolve?

Biologists would say *no*, because by definition only populations can evolve. But once we allow for forms of evolution that are not strictly biological, we can say that individuals evolve. Any parent can observe their children evolving intellectually, socially, morally, and ethically as they grow and participate in family life and society. A responsible parent, like your adult child, has self-evolved in all these areas far beyond the capacities they had when they were a two-year-old or a teenager.

45. What happens when we define *evolution* more broadly than biologists do?

Using natural selection, we can say the human species *Homo sapiens* has evolved mentally or intellectually over many thousands of years. In humanity's earliest days, no one could read, write, or do mathematics. Humanity has evolved since then through the evolution of education so that today most people on the planet can read, write, and do math. Even though there are still some people who do not possess these basic skills, the human species as a whole possesses them. These basic skills of reading, writing, and mathematics are examples of emergent properties developed by the human species. Furthermore, new abilities in each of these areas continue to occur, indicating that, intellectually, human beings have not reached their evolutionary limits.

Homo sapiens, the species, has developed other emergent properties using technology, including the ability to fly, travel underwater, print books, communicate worldwide, build huge cities, and trace our human history and the history of our planet. These are all stages of evolution produced through small changes over time.

46. What is *symbiosis* in biology?[3]

Symbiosis occurs whenever two organisms of different species exist in close physical contact, to the benefit of both organisms. Symbiosis can occur between animals, plants, fungi, or any combination thereof. Each organism contributes something that benefits the survival of the other, and in turn receives a survival benefit of its own. Any organism involved in symbiosis is called a *symbiote*.

Symbiosis, according to biologists, is an instinctive behavior of all living things driven by evolution. Some biologists might say that when symbiosis occurs, it is driven by natural selection, the evolutionary process identified and named by Charles Darwin. Many forms of symbiosis are discussed in biology textbooks.

Life on Earth probably wouldn't exist without symbiosis. Symbiosis is likely responsible for the evolution of all multicellular life, which includes just about every living thing. The theory that many new evolutionary forms of life are due to symbiosis is known as *symbiogenesis*.

This theory, now widely accepted, suggests that symbiosis is actually the key to the origins of all complex life on Earth. The theory says that many different kinds of microbes entered into a series of symbiotic relationships, with different microbes performing different tasks vital to microbial existence. As their symbiotic relationships grew more complex, they eventually evolved into a tightly integrated complementary network or system, each microbe contributing to the survival of the evolved system. The system of microbes eventually evolved a casing that enclosed them all, which is what we now call a living cell. Every living thing on Earth is made up of cells.

Our planet Earth is a symbiotic organism made up of countless different elements cooperating to maintain Earth's continued existence. These elements are not Earth, but elements of the symbiotic system we call Earth. Their combined activity and capacities interacting symbiotically all over the planet keep Earth surviving. In helping keep other people, animals, and plants alive, you are a planetary symbiote yourself.

Considered by itself, your body is a symbiotic organism made up of trillions of your own cells plus hundreds of other species of bacterial cells. These other species' cells are not you, but they survive because they live in your body, just as their activity throughout your body helps keep you surviving.

47. Can there be other forms of symbiosis that are not strictly biological?

The Jesuit scientist Pierre Teilhard de Chardin suggested that symbiosis may happen in the joining together of forms of existence other than cellular structures. He said that almost any two or more things can join together symbiotically so that their union becomes beneficial to the survival and development of each part. Thus symbiosis can happen in various areas of science and human society.

Symbiosis can happen in technology. Television may be seen as a symbiotic relationship between radio and film. A smartphone appears to provide a setting for many symbiotic relationships between its function as a telephone and the internet—and the countless apps that are available.

Symbiosis may occur among different sciences. The science of astrophysics describes a symbiotic relationship between astronomy and physics; similarly with astro-photography, paleobiology, physical chemistry, and so on.

An automobile may be viewed as a complex symbiotic relationship among many parts—wheels, steering, ignition, lighting, engine, lubrication, gears, seating, dashboard, computers—each of which depends on the proper functioning of all the other elements and on the survival of the auto itself.

Symbiosis in our modern world generates evolution most frequently—and quickly—through the mating of two or more different "parents," in almost any human activity.

48. Can you legitimately use symbiosis outside biology?

Although *symbiosis* was originally a biological term, meaning the union of two or more different life forms, it may easily be applied to various activities of *human life*, such as science, mathematics, technology, communication, transportation, entertainment, philosophy, theology, psychology, and so on. These fields are expressions of human life. None of them could have come into existence without human thought. As far as these different fields were originally invented with human biological brains, we could even claim that these scientific and artistic forms of symbiosis are "biological," because they require the complex neurology of one or more human biological brains for their existence and maintenance.

Thus, symbiosis may be used more broadly, not only to describe the joining of two different *life forms* (animal breeding), but also the joining of two different *technologies* (robotics and medical surgery), two different *fields of study* (astronomy and physics into astrophysics), two different *systems of thought* (evolutionary theory and Christian theology), and various *human relationships* (sports teams, research teams).

Once people identify the two methods of evolution, *natural selection* (mutation, gradual changes over generations) and *symbiosis*, they will naturally want to know the laws, principles, or forces that can help bring about natural selection and symbiosis.

There are four fundamental laws or forces governing evolution: *attraction, connection or union, complexity*, and *consciousness*. These laws were first identified and named by the Jesuit scientist Pierre Teilhard de Chardin; Teilhard, for short. Let's look at each force in turn.

49. What is the role of *attraction* in evolution?

Attraction is the basic force in the universe. It can initiate any evolutionary process, whether by mutation or symbiosis. Notice that the basic physical forces of the universe—gravity, electromagnetism, and nuclear cohesion—are all forces of *attraction*. They bring about evolution at the most elemental stages of the universe. For example, the evolution of *subatomic particles symbiotically joining to form atoms* created over one hundred new atoms—the gases, liquids, metals, and minerals listed in the Periodic Table of Chemical Elements. By the combined attractive forces of gravity and magnetism, the stars and planets evolved.

Next came the *symbiotic joining of different atoms to form molecules and compounds* (salts, water, acids, alkaloids, enzymes, proteins, and so on).

Next came the *symbiotic union of many different megamolecules to produce the living cell.*

From the symbiotic union of many, many cells, over millions of years, emerged the entire biological world of fish, plants, animals, and humans.

Animals and humans are very conscious of attraction, the force used to form friendships and mates. Among humans, attractive forces are not limited to sex and pleasure, but may be based on shared interests in science, literature, art, history, nature, entertainment, music, sports, technology, politics, causes, philosophy, religion, and a host of other things.

The basic purpose of all attractive forces is to bring different things together and to create connections or unions. On Earth, gravity keeps everything connected to the ground. As long as we remain on our planet, we can never escape having to deal with the effects of gravity and electromagnetism. A roller coaster at the fairgrounds creates excitement because of gravity. All the electronic software in the computer on your desk and in your cell phone obey the attractive (and repulsive) forces of electromagnetism.

The lesson to learn from this is that if you want to bring about evolution in any area, say, your family, your school, your workplace, your church, or even in yourself, *begin by using the powerful force of attraction. Learn what attracts people and use this force wisely.*

50. What is the role of *connection/union* in evolution?

Most people would never consider human connections (unions, relationships, teams, and so on) as having their own evolutionary power. Teilhard, however, recognized the dual role human unions or groups play in evolution.

First of all, Teilhard says that *unions are real entities* existing in the world. Unions are distinct from the members that make up the union.[4] Committed relationships and research teams are not only real in themselves, but they are also *examples of evolution* precisely because, as relationships, they are a working combination of various abilities and capacities that none of the individual members possesses. A basketball team is a real entity for it alone can "win a game" (an emergent property). None of the individual players can do what a team can do.

Teilhard's point is that *unions have a life of their own.* A family *as a union* has a life and dynamics of its own distinct from the lives and emotional dynamics of its individual family members. A sports team has a life and purpose of its own, distinct from the private lives and purposes of the individual team members. Even when a team, say, a high school sports team, loses some of its senior members and replaces them with other students, fans and alumni still relate to the team as a living unit having its own identity.

51. How do unions help their individual members to evolve?

Teilhard also noticed that a true union (friendship, marriage, sports team, research team, and so on) does not absorb its members or dilute them. Rather, their involvement in the team or union evokes in them qualities and abilities that might otherwise never have been recognized or developed.

Musicians improve their talent and performance skills by playing in a professional band or orchestra. This way, each musician in the group develops sensitivity to other personalities, learns cooperation, self-discipline, patience, and skill in listening. In other words, as Teilhard put it, "Union differentiates," that is, in a true union the individuals in the union become more of themselves than they would or could have become by themselves. Thus, a true union or relationship challenges its members to evolve.

The lesson to be learned is *Evolution happens within relationships. So, to foster evolution, form true, committed relationships.*

52. What is the role of *complexity* in evolution?

Complexity in our lives is an effective force for bringing about evolution among human beings. It challenges us to enlarge our consciousness in order to make sense of the complexity. For example, most committed relationships into which we enter add a level of complexity to our lives that was not there before. Our mind is challenged to integrate the new relationship into our other relationships and our other commitments. Such integration is the work of consciousness.

As an example, suppose I join a book discussion group, and the preparatory assignment is to read chapter 1. During discussions at the group meeting, I quickly discover that other members have a variety of responses to the reading, some of which may be different from my interpretation of the chapter. I also discover that I need to open my mind to accommodate the complex variety of differing opinions and perspectives in the group, if I want to enter into a discussion.

Most of us don't like to add any new complexity into our lives. We resist it. But attraction—to a person, a puppy, a sport, a new experience—often overrides our resistance to complexity and brings us into new relationships or groups that add complexity to our lives. This is nature's way of continuing to challenge us to keep evolving personally.

To integrate a new complexity into our lives without compartmentalizing it requires an expansion of consciousness. The lesson to be learned is *Complexity triggers consciousness, the gateway to personal and shared evolution.*

53. What is the role of *consciousness* in evolution?

Trying to deal successfully with complexity stretches our consciousness and forces us to enlarge and expand our view of reality. Thus, we evolve personally and collectively. Compassion is enlarged. Knowledge grows. Personalities are enriched. Openness to other new things widens. "Vision" and perceptions expand and open up. People learn to see things they could never otherwise see, notice, or recognize. They establish new connections and produce new complexity.

Consciousness allows us to open our hearts to compassion, forgiveness, and love. It enables us to see potential in ourselves and others that we could not have seen before.

When enough people share a new level of consciousness, humanity itself may evolve. For example, early in the twentieth century humanity became aware of a need for a world government, a world court of justice, a world health organization, a world economy, a universal respect for human rights, a coordinated system for dealing with food crises and pandemics worldwide, an awareness that human behavior affects the health and life of the planet, a need for the human race to think and act as a unity.

Each of these developmental elements of our collective life mark the beginnings of a new stage in human evolution, seeing the planet as one giant living organism that needs to stay healthy and grow. Each stage can only be attained or accomplished by a shared universal consciousness. As each of these planetary organizations mature in their effectiveness, humanity will come to possess a new kind of wisdom that our species has never yet known or experienced.

The lesson to be learned is *Evolution happens by expanding consciousness and sharing consciousness.*

54. Why complexity and consciousness?

Complexity is important because it may be used as a way to measure the path of evolution over time. Using measurement by *complexity*, we can trace and measure the evolution of the universe from its simplest beginnings as particles of inert matter through the emergence of life forms. Throughout this process, new "species" appear with steadily increasing complexity. An animal's nervous system is far more complex than that of any plant, and the human nervous system is far more complex than that of animals.

We can also trace the evolutionary stages of the universe from the moment of the Big Bang in terms of *consciousness*. Over time, living creatures show a clear parallel pattern of continual increasing neural complexity and expanded consciousness. These two factors, complexity and consciousness, appear to clearly identify evolution's direction.

Signs of Evolution

55. What does it mean to evolve?

We can say that something has evolved if it meets the following four requirements: It must:

1. Be something new that was not here before.
2. Have "parents," that is, it can be traced to an earlier source(s).
3. Possess new qualities, abilities, or characteristics that its predecessors or parts did not have.
4. Typically, be more complex than any of its parts.

56. How early in the universe did things start evolving?

Right after the Big Bang, in the first moments of the universe, there were only countless subatomic particles. With the emergence of the earliest atoms (hydrogen and helium), huge collections of them under gravitational forces (forces of attraction) helped form the first stars.

The appearance of stars in the young universe qualifies as an evolutionary event because stars fulfill the four requirements of evolution:

1. Before the first stars appeared, there was *nothing like them* in the universe. There were only numberless simple atoms floating in space.
2. Billions of these *parental atoms* came together under the forces of attraction. They produced a single magnificent union that qualified as a star. Our sun is a star.

3. These magnificent unions called stars had a number of *new properties or abilities* that their atom "parents," lacked. One emergent property was the ability to generate light and heat. Another was the ability to move in a fixed orbit. Stars also developed an ability, using the forces of attraction and union with hydrogen and helium, that enabled other more complex elements like carbon and oxygen to come into existence.
4. Stars were certainly *more complex* in their makeup than any atoms found within the star. Therefore, stars filled the four conditions to qualify as evolved objects in the universe.

57. Is evolution a continuing process in the universe?

Yes. The early universe continued to evolve by using the forces of attraction and union. These forces helped form more complex chemical unions, each one qualifying as a new entity in the world. The atoms hydrogen and helium are early examples. Each new chemical that formed qualified as an evolutionary event because each chemical had its own abilities and properties. Some newly formed atoms had the properties of gases, others of liquids, others of minerals, others of metals. Eventually, chemical evolution would produce over a hundred of these new elements. They are listed in the Periodic Table of Chemical Elements, familiar to every high school chemistry student. Insects, like mosquitoes, continue to evolve. The COVID-19 virus evolved many times in just a few years.

58. Does the original definition of *evolution* hold true for intellectual and technological innovations?

Yes. Evolution in intellectual and technological fields may still be identified using the same four conditions. Evolution can happen to an idea, a system, a species, a field of study, or a process. The evolved thing must be (1) genuinely new, (2) have parents, (3) possess new abilities or qualities that its "parents" did not possess, and (4) be more complex than any of its parts.

A simple example of intellectual evolution is mathematics. Over many thousands of years, mathematics continued to evolve from mere counting on one's fingers to the four basic skills of arithmetic (addition, subtraction, multiplication, division). These four became the original parents for all future fields of mathematics. Over the centuries, arithmetic evolved successively into fractions, decimals, geometry, algebra, calculus, logarithms, complex functions, set theory, statistics, et cetera. At each evolved stage, new mathematical abilities, or capacities to calculate, appeared that each previous stage of mathematics did not possess. And none of the functions or capabilities of previous "parents" has been lost or done away with. The most sophisticated forms of mathematics today still use the basic four skills of arithmetic.

59. How pervasive is evolution?

The simple answer is that evolution permeates the universe. Evolution is far more expansive and all-encompassing than the evolution of physical, chemical, and biological organisms. Evolution includes all the fields of human endeavor, such as communication, transportation, technology, information storage, and medicine, as well as "systems of thought" such as philosophy, ethics, culture, and theology. Human beings seem driven to have new ideas and create new things. *Humanity keeps trying to evolve because it is built into our DNA.*

60. Is evolution merely a theory?

Evolution is not merely a theory, a system, or a hypothesis. It is the principle that underlies the growth and development of all things on Earth and in the cosmos. It is the principle that brought about and explains almost everything that has happened in the universe. The drive to evolve—to attract and connect in ever-new ways—was built into the universe from its beginnings.

Evolution is the overriding process that permeates everything in the universe. The entire story of the universe is centered on and driven by the forces of evolution.

In fact, because evolution has been found everywhere in the universe and has always been happening, evolution has come to be recognized as a distinct and essential *dimension* of all reality in the cosmos. The universe cannot be understood without it. Evolution is not the problem; it is the solution.

In John Paul II's 1996 message to the Pontifical Academy of Sciences, he said as much:

> Today, almost half a century after publication of the encyclical [*Humani Generis*], new knowledge has led to the recognition of the theory of evolution as more than a hypothesis. It is indeed remarkable that this theory has been progressively accepted by researchers, following a series of discoveries in various fields of knowledge. The convergence, neither sought nor fabricated, of the results of work that was conducted independently is in itself a significant argument in favor of the theory.[5]

61. Does evolution have a direction or purpose?

A century ago, most scientists believed that evolution had no clear direction, that its movements were random and without any ultimate purpose. Current cumulative data of evolutionary events offer evidence that suggests otherwise.

Of course, sometimes evolution happens by chance, random movement, or trial and error, not only in the biological world but also in the world of ideas. Every inventor, artist, or research scientist reports experiences of trial and error and random success. None of this can refute the evidence that evolution in the long term has been moving in an identifiable direction. From a multibillion-year perspective, evolution's direction and purpose might be described as *continued growth in complexity and consciousness.*

62. How do we know when evolution has happened?

Evolution can come about in two basic ways:

1. Something new appears on Earth that was not here before, or
2. Something that was here before has gone through a series of small changes over time that add up to a significant change, so that it can now perform in ways that it never could before.

An example of the first way of evolving—*something new that had never been here before*—might be the invention of the alphabet and writing. Before cuneiform script was created in Mesopotamia about 3200 BCE, people counted and recorded goods with clay tokens. Writing was a new and different method of accounting.[6]

An example of evolution's second way—*through a series of small mutations*—might be the computer chip. Significant leaps in memory storage, miniaturization, and speed of operation have made today's computer chips able to do things they could never do before, such as store immensely more amounts of information, even an entire Hollywood film on one tiny flash drive. Yet they are still "computer chips."

The simplest way to recognize that evolution has happened is when some creature or idea or system or discovery or thing appears that *possesses qualities or abilities or properties that were not present in anything that went before*. These new abilities are called "emergent properties."

For example, Galileo's telescope possessed a capacity for seeing at a great distance. This emergent property of his telescope gave us the *new knowledge* that our sun was not a satellite of planet Earth, but that Earth was a satellite of the sun. This new knowledge enabled us to understand cosmology better and to get a more accurate perception of our solar system. Earth is just one of a number of planets orbiting around the sun. Only with this information were scientists able to plot the orbits of the planets and accurately calculate their distance from the sun.

63. Do emergent properties continue to appear? Where do they come from?

Whenever you can identify emergent properties in something, you are likely to be dealing with evolution. In technology, today's smart phone is an evolution beyond the landline phone and even beyond the mobile phone and the cell phone because, as a handheld communications device, the smart phone possesses new emergent properties capable of many new abilities that earlier phones did not possess; it can take pictures, make videos, access the Internet, play music, play games, and operate many other apps. Things or creatures with new abilities do not appear out of nowhere. Everything that is born or appears as new on Earth has "parents."

Various hominid species are evolved descendants of the primates. Human beings have not lost any of the social advances made by the primates, such as their ability to form a community and to care for and protect each other. In turn, human beings have discovered and invented new forms of relating that enhance life, such as schools, hospitals, communication systems, and so on.

Albert Einstein is an intellectual descendant of physicists of an earlier age. His discoveries about gravity, for instance, do not do away with the earlier work of Galileo, Kepler, Bacon, or Newton, but it enriches them.

64. Can a person "believe" in evolution?

Practically speaking, to believe in evolution means to acknowledge the prevalence of evolution in all of life. A person who believes in evolution and acts to foster evolution is *evolutive*.[7] Such a belief allows—and requires—you to think and act evolutively. Once you put on an evolutive mindset, you can begin to consciously recognize and acknowledge evolution whenever it happens. You desire to develop knowledge of the laws of evolution and learn to bring a sense of openness to evolution into your daily life. You can teach others how to use the laws of evolution personally and socially in order to help humanity move in a forward evolutionary way.

65. What is the future of evolution?

Evolution has been occurring steadily since the first moments of space/time. With the advent of *Homo sapiens*, people have enjoyed the capacity and the drive to continue the forward march of evolution, sometimes consciously and often unconsciously. That is, someone may invent a new technology that allows human evolution to move forward, while the inventor of this new technology was motivated by monetary profit, unaware of his contribution to fuller human life.

In Christian tradition, the most important direction for human evolution lies in our ability to grow in human love. Jesus's vision for humanity was for our species to learn to love, to develop higher ways of loving, so that our entire human family could become one family enveloped in love and contributing to that love.

Because of their belief structure, Christians are in the best position to consciously design evolutionary products that not only move evolution "forward" but also "upward," toward human unity based on love for one another.

66. What is God's relation to evolution?

Because everything in creation is driven to evolve, and God loves what God created, it seems clear that God loves evolution. We may also say that God is Love, and that divine love created an evolving universe, one that is evolving in its ability to love unconditionally, universally, and in fullest consciousness. God wants us to evolve in consciousness and in our ability to love unconditionally so that, when eventually we encounter God directly, we may more fully grasp the divine nature and be transformed into it.

PART 3

CHRISTIANITY

An Evolutionary Religion

Our experience makes it perfectly clear that, *during the course of evolution*, emergence happens only successively and in mechanical dependence on what precedes it.

Teilhard de Chardin[1]

Christianity as an Evolutionary Religion

67. Is it against my Christian faith to believe in evolution?

Not at all. In fact, Christianity itself began as an evolutionary religion. From Jesus's teachings and throughout its many centuries, the church and its members have been forerunners in enhancing the human condition and enlarging human consciousness. The church's many tenets and doctrines require a transformation (evolution) of each believer's mindset and way of seeing the world and God's relationship to the world. All of these advances in Christian theology mark evolutionary steps in theology and faith.

68. What is an example of a Christian doctrine that has evolved?

Christianity has evolved our understanding of the nature of God. The Christian understanding of God is new. This understanding goes far beyond the beliefs about and descriptions of God or gods in earlier civilizations, such as Egyptian, Persian, Indian, Hebrew, Greek, Roman, and so on. It calls for you to reenvision or evolve any previous notions of God.

Christians are called to see:

- God as unconditionally loving, full of compassion and forgiveness.
- God as wanting the fullness of life for every creature.
- God as three divine persons in one nature.
- Jesus Christ as fully human and fully divine.

- Jesus Christ as Head of a universal (cosmos-sized) body and ourselves as physical parts of Christ's Universal Body.
- The Eucharist as the living presence of Christ's Universal Body.

These Christian beliefs, and others, require believers to evolve their intellects, their consciences, and their levels of consciousness.

69. How has Christianity contributed to the evolution of the human species?

The primary characteristic of a species that has evolved is that many, if not most, members of a species have capacities and abilities that the species from which it evolved never had.

Over time, human beings continued to evolve, not so much biologically, as socially, emotionally, intellectually, technologically, and spiritually. Humanity evolved from hunter-gatherers into farmers, herders, artisans, and traders. Nomadic tribes began to create permanent settlements. People developed societies and governments, commerce, art forms, clothing, spoken and written languages, mathematics, and medicine. All of those factors are forms of our species evolving, but our evolution has not stopped.

Instead of seeing religion as an insignificant force in the evolution of *Homo sapiens*, religion, especially Christianity, has functioned as a prime mover in humanity's evolutionary journey. The clear evidence of this fact has often been overlooked and neglected by science.

From its earliest days, core Christian beliefs evolved the moral standards of the human family. For example, Christianity taught that all persons were equal and had the right to life—to be loved, welcomed in society, and treated justly. Because Christians believed that God was a God of love and compassion, Christianity charted a new direction for humanity and a new level of relating and interrelating. Its moral principles initiated an evolutionary leap in the human phenomenon, although no one at that time would have called it by that name. Christians welcomed into their ranks—and cared for—the poor, the sick, widows, orphans, lepers, outcasts, slaves. They welcomed to the eucharistic table everyone who believed in Jesus Christ.

In the centuries following the beginnings of Christianity, Christians were at the forefront of many fields that affected the continuing evolution of humanity, most especially education. Christians promoted basic education for all, and eventually education became a core value among nations, as well as university education for those ready for it. Because of Christian initiatives, education became the engine of ingenuity, discovery, and evolution on our planet.

Medieval monasteries collected and preserved manuscripts, such as scientific, mathematical, and philosophical works written in Hebrew, Greek, and Latin and, later on, in Arabic. These monks could be credited for maintaining the richness of the body of human knowledge and skills, which included religious and philosophical learning as well as information about science, history, medicine, drama, poetry, philosophy, religion, and mathematics, material that would otherwise have been lost forever.

Monasteries also preserved classical crafts and artistic skills as centers where new forms of music developed, new musical instruments were created, and musical notation was invented. They also functioned as agricultural, economic, and production centers, particularly in remote regions, thus becoming major conduits for the growth of Western civilization. Monasteries introduced new technologies and new crops, energy supply, food preparation, wine making, and herbal medicine. In all these ways, they promoted economic growth.

Each of the innovations introduced by people living Christian values helped *Homo sapiens* take many small evolutionary steps forward in human development. Innovations created by these men and women of faith flowed from their Christian commitment, following Jesus's example, of building the kingdom of God on Earth. "Thy will be done on earth...."

70. How do we identify evolution happening in the human race?

Remember, to scientifically observe and continually track the growth of human evolution, it is not enough to trace evolutionary events that are merely biological. Human evolution cannot be studied separately from evolution happening in all human fields: in science, mathematics, technology, communication, transportation, education, art, and so on.

The simplest way to recognize that evolution has happened is when some creature or idea or system or discovery or thing appears that *possesses qualities or abilities or properties that were not present in anything that went before.* These new abilities are called "emergent properties." They include new knowledge, new techniques, new technology, new systems, new concepts, new insights, new fields of study, new social structures, and the like.

One has only to trace the history of human communication to recognize the series of emergent properties that have continued to appear in the field of personal communication over time—from the written letter to the telegraph to the telephone to the mobile phone to the cell phone to the smart phone, to the internet, to social media. At each new stage, each new communication tool manifests new properties that were not available to human life before. Many people today cannot imagine human life without a smart phone. Yet a hundred years ago, there wasn't a human on the planet who could even imagine such an instrument.

Christianity and Western Culture

71. What evolutionary role did Christianity play in the development of Western culture?

Christianity has played a prominent role in the development and evolution of Western cultural, scientific, and spiritual life. Christianity assimilated much from its birth parents: Jewish culture and the classical cultures of Greece and Rome. As Christianity grew, it added an evolutionary richness to the mix that was all its own. During its first fifteen hundred years, Christianity rapidly expanded the good news of its value system and its belief system throughout Asia, Africa, Europe, India, and the Americas.

According to historian Paul Legutko, the Catholic Church was "at the center of the development of the values, ideas, science, laws, and institutions which constitute what we call Western civilization."[2]

Throughout most of its history, Western culture has been nearly equivalent to Christian culture. Much of the population of the Western hemisphere could broadly be described as culturally Christian.[3]

Even atheists assimilated and upheld many of Christianity's basic values and ethical principles. These included respect for every person's life, a commitment to improving the quality of life for all, a philanthropic spirit, universal education, the advancement of science, cultivation of the arts, protection of the rights of workers, the equality of women, nonviolence, rejection of racism, protection of children, individual rights, free speech, and freedom to worship—or not.

For at least seventeen hundred years, Christianity remained the dominant force guiding the course of philosophy, literature, and theology. Throughout Western civilization, it planted a belief in monotheism and access to a loving God. It valued the life of every human being and, as a missionary church, hoped to create a better future for all humankind. Wherever Christian missionaries went, they provided education and health care to the people they served as well as offering Christian doctrine.

Christianity also had its "shadow" side. For example, in the United States, Christianity was used to justify the centuries-long legal institution of enslavement of African people, the genocide in North America of many Native American tribes by the "Christian" settlers under the banner of "Manifest Destiny," the forced conversion to Christianity of many native peoples and African slaves throughout South, Central, and North America, the subjugation of women as inferior to men, and the antisemitism that eventually gave rise to the Holocaust. Much of the shadow side of Christianity that has infected Western civilization during the last five centuries may find its roots in the pernicious, pervasive, and unfounded belief in the privileges of white males—their supremacy, entitlement, and dominance.

Nevertheless, as a missionary church, its teachings also had a strong impact on marriage and family life wherever Christianity took hold. It played a role in ending practices common among pagan societies, such as human sacrifice, slavery, infanticide, and polygamy.[4]

72. What evolutionary contributions did Christianity make to morality and ethics?

Two of Christianity's more important contributions to humanity's evolving moral system were its focus on the *value of all life* and the *equality of all people*. Christianity's care for and equal—if not special—treatment of the poor, the sick, widows, orphans, servants, and slaves brought about major evolutionary steps in respect for human life. These values were enshrined in Jesus's teachings in his Sermon on the Mount and preserved in the church's founding documents, namely, the books of the New Testament. Evidence of these values being put into practice among early believers may be found in the Acts of the Apostles and the letters of St. Paul. They described life in early Christian communities in the Middle East and Europe.

For example, thanks especially to St. Paul, Christianity brought about new roles in leadership for women. In Christian gatherings, women appeared alongside men as members with full rights who used their charismatic gifts within the congregation. In the letters of Paul, women were mentioned as leaders of equal value. Paul addressed Prisca (Priscilla) as his fellow worker (Rom 16:3). The four daughters of Philip were active as prophets in the congregation (Acts 21:8–9). Pagan critics of the church, such as Porphyry (234–305), even suggested that women ruled the church. During periods of Christian persecution, women as well as men showed great courage in their suffering. The fact that women were honored as martyrs and mentioned by name in the eucharistic liturgy demonstrated their active roles in the churches.[5]

73. What evolutionary contributions did Christianity make to medicine and health care?

One of the first evolutionary movements that may be attributed to Christianity occurred in health care. Christianity was the first religious institution—or secular state—to build hospitals to care for the sick poor. Hospitals from the Byzantine Empire, described as large complexes, resembled the beginning of what we now know as modern hospitals.[6] Most were designed for the poor and were almost exclusively utilized by the poor. They also provided safe and caring places to ease death for the chronically or terminally ill.[7] Hospitals and other institutions of care spread across the empire.

During the Middle Ages, the church administered hospitals for the elderly and orphanages for the young, hospices for the sick of all ages, places for lepers to live safely, and hostels or inns where pilgrims could find an inexpensive bed and meal. The church supplied food to the population during famine and distributed food to the poor. It funded this welfare system by collecting taxes on a large scale and by the renting of large farmlands and estates.[8] These places of health care and refuge were often connected to monasteries and run by monks.

During Europe's Age of Discovery and Exploration, beginning in the fifteenth century, Catholic missionaries introduced the European sciences to India, China, and Japan. They also provided health care and education to the people there. In Asia, the church became a major provider of health care services, especially in Catholic nations like the Philippines. Christian health care services continued to spread and increase, so that today the Roman Catholic Church is the largest nongovernmental provider of health care services in the world.[9]

74. What evolutionary contributions did Christianity make to education?

From their earliest days, monasteries maintained large copying rooms called *scriptoria*, where monks preserved important books and manuscripts by making handwritten copies and distributing them. These collections of scrolls and books became the first Christian libraries.

During the Dark Ages, monasteries continued their educational function of building libraries and teaching. Monasteries also ran schools for externs. Until the rise of universities in big cities, these monasteries, convents, and cathedrals operated virtually all schools and libraries in Europe. In many towns, these schools, the forerunners of future universities, date back to the sixth century.[10]

The Catholic Church also founded many of the early and most influential universities in England, Europe, and North America.

The medieval universities of Western Christendom were well integrated across Western Europe, all of them using Latin as a shared intellectual language. These institutes of higher learning encouraged freedom of inquiry and produced a wide variety of fine scholars and natural philosophers. One of these was St. Albert the Great (1200–80), a Dominican friar, who is considered a pioneer of biological field research.[11] He studied at the University of Padua and spent much of his time teaching at the University of Paris.

The Catholic Church has always been involved in evolving formal education. Missionary activity for the Catholic Church has always incorporated education of evangelized peoples as part of its social ministry. History shows that in evangelized lands, the first people to operate schools were Roman Catholics. In some countries, the church remained the main provider of education or significantly supplemented government forms of education.[12]

In a word, the church created the basis of the Western system of education, one of the greatest contributions to evolutionary growth in all intellectual disciplines.

According to records, the number of Catholic educational units worldwide in the year 2000 included 120,000 primary and secondary schools with 6,980 in the United States, as well as over 1,000 colleges and universities in 100 different countries, with 244 colleges in the United States. In 2016–17, Catholic schools formed the largest private (K–12) school system in the United States.[13]

75. How important is learning in the evolutionary process?

From the perspective of evolution, education serves as the major evolutionary force operating among all living species. Education is so widespread a phenomenon, so ordinary and clearly visible everywhere that there seems to be no reason to look for any mystery in it. After all, education is an acknowledged universal biological function throughout the living world. It is well known that all animals learn, accumulate, and transmit learned experiences and skills, old and new, to their young through example, modeling, practice, and training.

In human evolution, education fosters the evolution not merely of individuals but of our entire species. Evolution has always been aimed at enriching *Homo sapiens* as a whole, not just individuals.

The specific function of education among human beings is to maintain the *evolution of the species*. It was

> to extend and ensure in collective mankind a consciousness which may have already reached its limit in the individual. Its fulfillment, in the case of humanity, of this specific function is the final proof of the biological nature and value of education, extending to things of the spirit.[14]

76. What evolutionary contributions did Christianity make to philosophy and theology?

The primary thrust of early Christian philosophy was to build a philosophical foundation to support the Christian religious message.[15] Although Greek philosophers such as Plato and Aristotle evolved their fields beyond what went before, Christian philosophers and theologians were faced with unique theological, metaphysical, and ethical challenges. They believed their leader, Jesus Christ, was both fully human and fully divine, and that he had resurrected from the dead. In his sermons, Jesus said to his followers, you should be willing to die for your friends, you are to love your enemies, do good things to those who hate you, and forgive again and again those who offend you, up to seventy-seven times. Explaining these doctrines and teachings required the integration of philosophy and theology, including logic, ethics, and cosmology.

Some of the earliest Christian theologians and philosophers (150–500)[16] were challenged to evolve philosophical and theological concepts as the community of disciples adapted to Gentile converts, Roman persecutions, and the spread of Christianity throughout the Roman Empire. They developed responses to issues of evil, sin, suffering, death, resurrection, marriage, love, friendship, worship, community, human nature, divine nature, reason and faith, spirituality, miracles, heaven, hell, obedience, sacrifice, baptism, Eucharist, divine revelation, civic and religious authority, the role of women, and care for the poor and the sick.

Christian theologians and philosophers in the early medieval period (500–1100)[17] had to deal with the collapse of the Roman Empire, and the emergence of the Holy Roman Empire when the pope held supreme secular power. The Crusades and the desire to reclaim the Holy Land for Christians raised new moral issues. It was also a time for the exploration of Christian love, friendship, devotion to Our Lady, the building of the great cathedrals, and the renovation of monastic life.

Christian theologians and philosophers in the High Medieval period (1100–1450)[18] faced the rise of the great European universities, the evolution of philosophy, the rediscovery of the Greek language, the Greek Fathers, and Islamic writings. Aquinas rewrote Christian theology using Aristotle's metaphysical concepts and his rules of logic (induction and deduction) to prove theological truths. Jorge Gracia argued that "in intensity, sophistication, and achievement, the philosophical flowering in the thirteenth century could be rightly said to rival the golden age of Greek philosophy in the fourth century B.C."[19]

Christian theologians and philosophers in the Renaissance (1450–1800) evolved new philosophical and theological perspectives due to the Protestant Reformation and the Catholic Counter-Reformation, the Council of Trent and Galileo's assertion that the sun does not revolve around Earth, challenging the cosmology proposed in the Book of Genesis. Descartes discovered the power of rational thinking and the use of evidence to prove a thesis. Henry VIII left the Roman Catholic Church and started his own Church of England.

Christian theologians and philosophers in the Late Modern period (1800–1950)[20] reinterpreted earlier ideas to account for the discoveries of modern science, including evolution. Industrialization that resulted in long working hours and poor working conditions led to the rise of workers' unions and the Catholic social teachings. With the emergence of new democracies, people's revolutions and revolts, Marxism, fascism, communism, atheism, atheistic philosophies, two world wars, the Holocaust, and nuclear warfare, new philosophical and theological questions demanded answers.

Christian theologians and philosophers in the second half of the twentieth century and the beginning of the twenty-first century[21] are evolving their thinking to deal with new understandings of the human person due to the rise of psychiatry and psychological theories. Ecumenism and interfaith dialogue are reshaping relationships with other faith traditions. A new awareness of racism, ageism, sexism, and feminism call for new understandings of inclusion and leadership. Medical procedures such as organ transplants, in vitro fertilization, contraception, and abortion raise new ethical questions. Issues of animal species extinction, global warming, and pollution have generated a rethinking of humanity's role in the world. Questions on the family and marriage are being reconsidered due to the increase of divorce, the emphasis on LGBTQ rights, and a greater understanding of domestic abuse. Violence and sexuality in film, pornography, addiction, pedophilia, and the clergy sexual abuse scandal demand new responses. Technologies such as the internet, social media, and cell phones raise questions that never before existed.

Through the centuries and continuing today, men and women philosophers and theologians have made innumerable evolutionary advances in the fields of philosophy, theology, metaphysics, logic, cosmology, and ethics.

Teilhard de Chardin in his book *The Human Phenomenon* implied that discoveries of science could provide a valuable source of divine revelation, or at least a clarification or enrichment of scriptural revelation. Theologically, Teilhard's discovery of evolution's universal pervasiveness showed that, in the beginning, God created, not a fixed and perfect universe according to the Book of Genesis, but an evolving and perfectible universe. Thus, God needed human cooperation, including continued scientific research, to help foster the development of the "kingdom of God" on Earth.

77. What evolutionary contributions did Christianity make to art?

Within Christianity's first few centuries, Christians introduced many new styles of artistic painting, such as manuscript illumination, icon painting, stained glass, and new layers of symbolism. They developed new colors, and new surfaces for painting, and later created oil paints. In the West at least, the history of art is the history of Christian art.

Illuminated manuscripts. During the early medieval period, Irish monastic art was dominated by the making of illuminated manuscripts, notably the stunning Book of Kells (800). These were handwritten books with detailed painted decorations that generally included flecks of precious metals such as gold or silver. Monks evolved many new techniques that were previously unknown to artists. Among these new skills were the art of preparing the vellum for illustration, the art of making quill pens, the art of preparing pigments for bright colors, the art of making the miniature artwork shine (thus the name "illuminated"), and the use of prepared egg yolk mixed with the paint to make the paint stick to the paper.[22] All of these advances marked small evolutionary movements in art.

Stained glass. In Europe, stained-glass windows were a major form of medieval pictorial art that has survived to this day. Evolving the art of creating the stains for the various colors of glass took years of experimentation, to the benefit of glaziers today. Contemporary stained-glass artists in the mid-nineteenth century, such as Charles Tiffany and his son Louis, benefited from the many evolutionary discoveries of medieval glaziers.[23]

Perspective in painting. The discovery of how to create *perception of space* in paintings, both linear and atmospheric perception, was another evolutionary step in artwork invented by Christians. *Linear perspective* involved using smaller figures to make things appear to be farther away.[24] *Aerial (or atmospheric) perspective* is another technique used primarily in landscape painting to suggest distance or depth using graduated color to represent the visual effects of atmosphere at different distances.[25]

Oil painting. During the fifteenth century, Jan van Eyck (1422–41) developed oil painting by mixing linseed oil and oil from nuts with different colors.[26] The invention of oil painting was another major evolutionary event that remains a significant medium among painters to this day.

78. What evolutionary contributions did Christianity make to literature?

The list of Catholic authors and literary works that have contributed to the evolution of literature in the West is vast. The Christian literary tradition spans more than two millennia. Countless historical works may be listed as noteworthy in terms of their evolutionary influence on Western society. From within Christianity came several new literary forms.

Autobiography. From late antiquity, St. Augustine's book *Confessions*, which outlined his sinful youth and conversion to Christianity, is widely considered to be the first autobiography in Western literature. Augustine (354–430) profoundly influenced the coming medieval worldview.

Encyclopedia. The *Summa Theologica*, perhaps the first encyclopedia of theology, was composed between 1265 and 1274. It was the best-known work of Dominican monk Thomas Aquinas (1225–74). Although unfinished, it was considered one of the classics in the history of philosophy and one of the most influential works of Western literature. Aquinas, in a kind of tour de force, evolved the metaphysical terminology and logic of Aristotle to reinterpret Christian theology.

Epic poetry. Dante Alighieri (1265–1321) and his *Divine Comedy* demonstrated that epic poems could be used to show the depths of human emotions and motivations.

Science fiction. The English statesman and philosopher, Thomas More (1478–1535) wrote the seminal work *Utopia*, perhaps the first fictional satire about a perfect world. This book is perhaps the first in the genre of social-science fiction.

How-to books. Among the first of the how-to book writers, Jesuit founder Ignatius Loyola (1491–1556), a key figure in the Catholic Counter-Reformation, was the author of an influential self-directed book of meditations known as the *Spiritual Exercises*.

79. What evolutionary contributions did Christianity make to music?

Over the last two thousand years, Christian men's and women's religious orders have enriched the world of music with the creation of new musical forms, new musical instruments, new methods of musical transcription, and new sources of inspirations for vocal and instrumental music.

Choir music. Through the centuries, Catholic monks composed an enormous body of religious music and developed new forms of liturgical choir music, such as Gregorian chant and polyphony. They also invented ways to transcribe and preserve it.

Musical notation. The scholar and music theorist Isidore of Seville, in the early seventh century, pointed out that "unless sounds are held by human memory, they perish, because they cannot be written down."[27] By the middle of the ninth century a form of musical notation began to develop in monasteries in Europe for teaching Gregorian chant. The earliest surviving musical notation of this type, using block symbols known as *neumes,* may be found in the *Musica disciplina* of Aurelian of Réôme, from about 850.

The musical staff. Benedictine monks of the tenth century invented the four-line staff and used the *neumes* of Gregorian chant to represent notes. The founder of what is now considered the standard five-line music staff, used by all musicians today, was Guido d'Arezzo (991–1033), an Italian Benedictine monk.[28]

Musical notation developed by Christians during this period became a new universal language. It marked a major evolutionary step. It provided a symbolic written language that visually represented music played with instruments or sung by the human voice, including notation that indicated durations or absence of sound, such as rests.

Using musical staffs and notes, a composer could write compositions for several instruments or voices ("parts"). Copies could be shared locally or internationally. Originals could be kept for making future copies. In this way, libraries of musical scores (orchestrations) could be preserved permanently. Thanks to the standardized forms of written music, an enormous body of religious music—chant, polyphony, choral, keyboard, and orchestral—was composed for performance by groups of musicians and vocalists and reproduced again and again in the future.

Keyboard instruments. Musician monks and other mechanics in monasteries invented what came to be called the piano keyboard. It was another evolutionary advance in music because a keyboard instrument could serve either as a solo instrument or as accompaniment for a singer or a choir.

Thanks to the double staff, the *pipe organ* came to be a standard church instrument in Western Europe starting around the year 900. Other early keyboard instruments to utilize the double musical staff were the *harpsichord* and the *piano.* The piano was an evolutionary step beyond the harpsichord because a piano enabled a pianist, as desired, to modify the volume of a note or a passage of music for emphasis or dramatic effect—excellent examples of emergent properties that a harpsichord did not possess.

Stringed instruments. Another evolutionary stage in music was marked by the inventions of the violin, viola, and cello. Christians in Italy first made these incredibly versatile stringed instruments during the early sixteenth century.[29]

Brass instruments. Christians were also credited with the creation of brass instruments, such as the trumpet, French horn, and trombone. During the Renaissance brass instruments began to emerge that resembled modern brass instruments in use today. Heinrich Stölzel (1777–1844) is credited with affixing the first documented valve to the instrument we now call the French horn in 1814. Soon the valve system replaced the slide trumpet,[30] and composers began writing pieces for the valve trumpet.

Catholic composers. The list of Catholic composers and Catholic sacred music that hold a prominent place in Western culture is extensive.

80. What evolutionary contributions did Christianity make to science and mathematics?

Some of today's history of science scholars, such as Stanley Jaki, have claimed that Christianity, with its particular worldview, was a crucial factor for the emergence and evolution of modern science.[31] Some scholars and historians of science assert that Christianity contributed directly to the rise of the scientific revolution.[32]

Under the church's leadership, the number of universities as well as the pace of science grew rapidly throughout Europe in the eleventh and twelfth centuries. Most of the scientific and technological advances in Europe were made in monasteries in Europe and Ireland. Unfortunately, the names of individual monks who may have made these evolutionary discoveries were never recorded.[33]

By the thirteenth century, historians begin to identify individuals who helped science, technology, and mathematics evolve. These include Roman Catholic individuals, priests, laity, and later Protestants who made significant advances in their respective scientific fields.

81. Who were some of the Christian pioneers in the sciences?

Following is a sampling through the centuries of Christian pioneers in the sciences.

Thirteenth Century

Robert Grosseteste (1175–1253), English bishop and scholar, showed that light is essential to the creation and perpetuation of life on Earth.

Albertus Magnus (1193–1280), also known as Albert the Great, was a bishop, whose scientific and philosophical writings filled thirty-eight volumes in topics such as logic, botany, geography, astronomy, mineralogy, and zoology.

Roger Bacon (1220–92), a Franciscan friar, was an early advocate of the scientific method, who envisioned flying machines and motorized ships and carriages.

Fourteenth and Fifteenth Centuries

Nicole Oresme (1325–82), a bishop and counselor of King Charles V of France, invented today's very familiar xy–rectangular coordinates (the x-axis and y-axis), enabling scientists and statisticians to simultaneously geometrically graph the mutual relationship between two different variables.

Jean Buridan (1301–62), a parish priest, advanced the physics concept of inertia, correctly theorized that resistance of the air progressively reduces the impetus, and showed that weight can add or detract from speed.

Leonardo da Vinci (1452–1519) was famous for his far-reaching contributions to science, technology, anatomy, art, and design. His designs later helped us to invent things like the tank, the parachute, the helicopter, the calculator, and the double hull. He also described a rudimentary theory of plate tectonics.

Sixteenth Century

Nicolaus Copernicus (1473–1543), a Polish astronomer known as the father of modern astronomy, was the first modern European scientist to propose that Earth and other planets revolve around the sun and the heliocentric theory of the universe.

Christopher Clavius (1538–1612), Jesuit mathematician and astronomer, wrote textbooks that were used for astronomical classroom education in universities for over fifty years in and out of Europe. He promoted the adoption of a mathematics curriculum for all students.

Andreas Vesalius (1514–64), a Flemish doctor and distinguished medical scholar, is recognized as founder of the scientific study of anatomy by applying empirical methods of dissecting cadavers.

Seventeenth Century

The seventeenth century saw dramatic growth in science and mathematics. In addition to the more famous names such as *René Descartes*, *Johannes Kepler*, *Galileo Galilei*, and *Blaise Pascal*, some of the many scientists include:

Nicolas Steno (1638–86), a Catholic bishop, made notable contributions in paleontology and was often credited as giving birth to the sciences of geology and paleontology.

Giambattista Riccioli (1598–1671) and *Francesco Grimaldi* (1618–63) were both Italian Jesuit priests and astronomers who contributed to our knowledge of the moon. Grimaldi's map of the moon's surface now adorns the entrance to the National Air and Space Museum in Washington, DC.

Athanasius Kircher (1601–80), a Jesuit priest and scholar, was the first to map ocean currents, offer a comprehensive theory of volcanic eruptions, compile an encyclopedia on China, create a dictionary of the Coptic language, and write a book dedicated solely to acoustics.

Pierre de Fermat (1607–65), mathematician, made many contributions to number theory, optics, and analytic geometry. He founded modern number theory.

Eighteenth Century

Isaac Newton (1643–1727), the famous pioneer in mathematics, physics, and astronomy, is just one of many scientists of this century. Others include:

Roger Boscovich (1711–87), a physicist, astronomer, mathematician, and Jesuit priest, produced a precursor of atomic theory. He invented the first geometric procedure for determining the equator of a rotating planet.

Gottfried von Leibniz (1646–1716), metaphysician and logician, discovered the binary numeral system, or the base-2 system, which is used universally today in computers and related electronic devices.

Luigi Galvani (1737–98), an Italian physician and physicist, was a pioneer in electricity and was credited with the discovery of bioelectricity.

Antoine-Laurent Lavoisier (1743–94), a meticulous experimenter, so evolved the field of chemistry as to be called the father of modern chemistry.

Nineteenth Century

Bernard Bolzano (1781–1848), *Michael Faraday* (1791–1867), *Gregor Mendel* (1822–84), and *Henri Becquerel* (1852–1908) are just a few of the scientists and mathematicians in the nineteenth century. Other include:

Alessandro Volta (1745–1827) worked with electricity and connected his discoveries to chemistry and physics. His discoveries led to the subsequent age of electric power, such as the inventions of the electric battery, continuous current, and the hydrogen lamp.

André-Marie Ampère (1775–1836), a French physicist and pioneer in electricity, founded the science of electromagnetism.

Augustin-Louis Cauchy (1798–1857), a mathematician and prolific writer, helped lay the rigorous foundations of calculus. He pioneered the study of mathematical analysis.

Ányos Jedlik (1800–1895), a Benedictine priest, member of the Hungarian Academy of Sciences, is the unsung father of the dynamo and electric motor. In 1828, he built a small model of an electric car using a direct-current motor.

82. What changed among Catholic scientists in the twentieth century?

With Charles Darwin's (1809–82) discovery of evolution happening among living creatures everywhere on Earth, the Catholic Church took a defensive position toward science. The church's resistance to the theory of evolution began with Pope Leo XIII (1819–1903) and culminated in Pope Pius X's (1835–1914) 1907 encyclical *Pascendi Dominici Gregis* (On the Doctrines of the Modernists).[34] A few years later, in 1910, the pope issued a decree called The Oath Against Modernism.[35] All priests and teachers in Catholic seminaries and universities were required to publicly recite this entire oath against promoting modern science and evolution. The oath, in effect, proved disheartening to Catholic scientists,[36] especially those, like Teilhard de Chardin, who were discovering fossils of hominids that were evolutionary precursors of *Homo sapiens*.

83. Who were some of the significant Catholic scientists in the twentieth century?

Although the scientific community worldwide in general was bursting with scientific discoveries and advances during the twentieth century, the work of Catholic scientists visibly diminished. It is hard to find even a handful of Catholics in the forefront of the scientific world, a place they had held for the previous millennium. Here are a few.

Guglielmo Marconi (1874–1937), pioneer in wireless telecommunication, developed, demonstrated, and marketed the first successful long-distance wireless telegraph and in 1901 broadcast the first transatlantic radio signal.

Georges Lemaitre (1894–1966), a Belgian priest, astronomer, and cosmologist, was the first to propose the Big Bang Theory.

Ricardo Giacconi (1931–2018), Italian-born physicist, won the Nobel Prize for Physics in 2002 for his seminal discoveries of cosmic sources of x-rays, which helped lay the foundations for the field of x-ray astronomy.

Mario J. Molina (1943–2020), research chemist, proposed that chlorofluorocarbons (CFCs) had the potential to destroy the earth's protective ozone layer.

84. What will Christianity's role be in the evolution of humanity in the next centuries?

In 1950, Teilhard posed the all-important question regarding Christianity:

> Everyone is prepared to admit the importance of Christianity in the past; but what about the present? Surely, after two thousand years of existence the Christian movement (like so many others before it) must be showing signs of growing old and wearing out? Is the Christian God [like the morning sun] still climbing to the meridian—or is God not rather [like the evening sun] about to set on our horizon?[37]

Teilhard recognized that Christians, and specifically Catholic clergy, should be at the forefront of all evolutionary efforts toward human development because they should be aware of "Christ up Ahead" calling them forward.

Indeed, as the previous pages have made clear, Christians have made countless contributions to human progress in a broad and diverse range of fields, including medicine and health care, politics and government, literature and music, business and ethics, theology, philosophy and philanthropy, natural law and international law, science, and technology.

What will Christianity contribute to the future?

PART 4

CHRISTIANITY'S FUTURE

God has been leading us since the beginning of time, but now God includes us in the process of unfolding (Rom 8:28–30). This is the opportunity offered us as humans, and those who ride this Christ train are meant to be the "New Humanity" (Eph 2:15). Christ is both the Divine Radiance at the Beginning Big Bang and the Divine Allure drawing us into a positive future.

Richard Rohr[1]

At the present moment Christianity is the unique current of thought...which is sufficiently audacious and sufficiently progressive to lay hold of the world, at the level of effectual practice, in an embrace, at once already complete, yet capable of indefinite perfection, where faith and hope reach their fulfillment in love.

Teilhard de Chardin[2]

The Challenge Facing the Church

85. Can Christianity once again become an evolutive[3] church?

Hopefully, yes. However, as long as the Catholic Church and other Christian churches remain mired in a medieval cosmology and theology, these churches will become less and less significant in shaping the contemporary world. Science has undergone several major paradigm shifts since the Middle Ages, yet the church still relies on a medieval mindset to explain the faith.

For centuries, Christianity has presented itself as an "organized religion"—a institution that protects and promotes a system of beliefs that was handed down fully formed in the past. Yet Christianity's history of "tradition" is actually a story of change and adaptation. It has repeatedly tailored its message, methods, and mission to the changing fabric of civilization. Christianity at its core is creative, constructive, and evolutive.

86. What could the church do as a first step to regain its evolutive momentum?

If the church publicly introduced the fact that God created an evolving universe from the beginning, it would begin to evolve its theology, liturgy, and preaching. Things would begin to change. Each of these dimensions of the church—doctrine, morals, and liturgy—could then begin to develop an evolutionary perspective. Some of our prayers in the liturgy, which already have a built-in evolutionary perspective, would take on new meaning, for example, the Lord's Prayer.

From an evolutionary perspective, the promise we make every time we say the Lord's Prayer would take on a completely new meaning. Our prayer of desire—"Thy kingdom come. Thy will be done on earth"—is clearly written in the future sense. It is forward looking. We are aware that God's plan for humanity has not yet been fulfilled on Earth. In evolutionary language, humanity has not yet evolved enough for God's plan to be fulfilled.

In an evolutive church, each time we said the Lord's Prayer consciously, we would see ourselves promising to keep God's evolutionary project moving forward. Keeping God's mission moving forward through human effort would become a crucial factor in church life. An evolutionary perspective would become an essential part of promoting the kingdom of God on Earth. It would be a commitment to invent, create, build, and keep developing whatever was needed to bring Earth and everyone on it into the fullness of life, love, and unity.

87. What could the church's clergy and members do to show their commitment to an evolutionary mindset?

An evolutive church would publicly encourage young Christians, even clergy and consecrated religious, to aspire to careers that foster human evolution—in science, technology, communication, transportation, medicine, art, music, philosophy, theology, and especially education. We would develop a theology that stressed the value of human effort, a theology that would show how contributing to advancement in all of these fields was—and always has been—an integral part of Christian life.

Education will play a key role in promoting evolution because *education provides a way both to foster evolution as well as to recognize the direction in which human evolution is moving.* Teilhard said, "The sum of knowledge and acquirement retained and transmitted by education from one generation to the next constitutes a natural sequence from which the direction of evolution may be observed."[4] That "direction" of evolution, he said, might be best measured in terms of growth in complexity and consciousness, that is, in the enrichment of minds and spirits across the human race.

The two quotations opening this section envision an evolutive Catholic Church. They invite Christianity to formally take its place at the forward tip of the arrow of evolution, which is where God awaits us. Teilhard de Chardin says:

> Though frightened for a moment by evolution, the Christian now perceives that what it offers him is nothing but a magnificent means of feeling more at one with God, and of giving himself more to him.[5]

88. Are only Christians involved in furthering the evolutionary process?

Not at all. All human beings are on God's team, not just people of faith. God's project is one of creating global love and global unity. The question, "What is the future of Christianity?" must be considered in relation to other significant questions such as, "What is the future of humankind?" and "What is the future of our planet?"

For Christians, Jesus clearly stated God's evolutionary goal himself, "That they may be one, Father, as I am in you and you are in me, that they may be one in us" (John 17:11). Here, Jesus's vision and dream is a universal one. He is not describing a small religious sect whose members live in a loving union. He is asking his followers to help bring about an entire human race that will become a loving oneness in its totality. This is the planetary challenge Jesus proposed.

To achieve this goal, social justice objectives need to be accomplished, which will require everyone's help. Human health care needs to be continually improved. Living conditions need to be bettered—for people of every religion as well as for people without religion. Human well-being and the quality of work needs to be improved. The same goes for education, government, communication, transportation, and the many services that we rely on as human beings; they are all areas ripe for continual evolution.

Teilhard believed that the true function of religion is "to sustain and spur on the progress of life."[6] Religion is not meant to separate people, but to unite them in pursuit of what is good. God's evolutionary project involves all human beings. There can be no duality, division, or opposing teams in this project.

"Teilhard is one of the few modern thinkers on religion for whom evolution provided the dominant note of his entire work."[7] For him, the relationship between cosmos and religion is fundamental to the earth. In 1916, Teilhard wrote, "Religion and evolution should neither be confused nor divorced. They are destined to form one single continuous organism, in which their respective lives prolong, are dependent on, and complete one another, without being identified or lost....Since it is in our age that the duality has become so markedly apparent, it is for us to effect this synthesis."[8]

The church's job is to avoid division and encourage union. All human effort must be united for the success of this evolutionary project.

Moral Theology in a Future Church

89. If the church were to acknowledge that God from the beginning created an evolving universe, how would it affect Catholic moral theology?

Currently, the church's moral theology and metaphysics, as it has been from the beginning, assumes that we live in a static, or fixed, and complete universe, not an evolving one. The traditional basis of moral theology was that Earth is the unchanging center of the universe. Such a fundamental position is no longer tenable because its assumptions about Earth's cosmic status are not true and cannot continue to be used as the basis of making moral decisions or formulating doctrinal statements. Theologians need to acknowledge that the universe, including planet Earth, is incomplete and forever changing.

For example, in the eighteenth century, Isaac Newton, the greatest scientist and mathematician of his day, saw God's creation, the universe, as a giant clock. According to him, God just wound up the universe at the beginning of time and let it tick away through months and years in recurring cycles, like the hands of a clock going round and round. Since then, God has simply rested and watched the cosmic machinery do its thing. Newton's universal process was totally fixed and unchanging, which is how he assumed the universe was. We now know something fundamental that Newton did not know, namely, that our universe is evolving and expanding. It is a mystery far more awesome and revelatory of God's love and creativity than that of a slowly unwinding clock.

In traditional morality, based on a fixed and unchanging world like Newton's, "there is nothing new under the sun." Therefore, as long as moral theologians continue to see life on Earth as primarily a time of personal testing for entering heaven, *morality will continue to be seen as primarily an individual matter.* In this context, each individual is responsible for avoiding sin and staying in a state of grace. Before Vatican II, larger issues of social sin and social justice were not a focus of most people's moral concerns. In the late nineteenth century, popes published encyclicals promoting awareness of destructive social systems and the call to confront them. Yet seldom was awareness of social sins a topic of Sunday homilies, nor was it found on lists for examination of conscience before confession.

One was expected to be kind to others, especially the poor, the sick, and the troubled. Otherwise, Christian life was focused on forgiveness of personal sins and getting into heaven. Human work was something people did to earn a living and pay bills. Few went to work in an effort to change the world. Many toiled at boring or backbreaking jobs simply in the hope that their children would have a better life than they had.

90. What would an evolutionary ethics look like? What would be some of its guiding principles?

First, ethics would assume a universe in evolution moving toward higher complexity and more inclusive consciousness. Second, its moral principles would apply to relationships, groups, teams, and nations as well as to individuals.

The following moral and ethical principles of an evolutionary ethic were derived from Teilhard's writings. They provide a basic guide for evolutive persons and groups making moral and ethical decisions and actions.[9]

Ethical Principle 1. *Ethics is about guiding human choices and behavior in such a way that choices are made with the intention of making a positive difference in helping promote and advance God's evolutionary project.*

Actions and choices that make a positive difference in human life form the core of moral and ethical living in an evolutionary world. These choices and actions would affect the lives of self and others, the welfare of the community, and the health of the planet.

God's project involves transforming the world in love.[10] Our job as moral persons is to join together in this grand work for love of God and God's creation. Standing by and watching others do the transformational work is not an acceptable alternative.[11]

Ethical Principle 2. *An evolutionary ethics is focused on each person and group taking positive action to make a positive difference, alone and with others.*

Every day, moral and ethical decisions and actions—made by individuals, groups, organizations, or nations—may be large or small. They may involve simple interactive behaviors of caring and compassion as well as major decisions that affect large numbers of people. Each action, large or small, intending to make a positive difference in the world contributes to God's project as long as it is done with goodwill.

For many, this is a new way of looking at their moral and ethical life. A moral life is no longer focused on avoiding sin, but on *making a positive difference.*

Ethical Principle 3. *The moral call is for individuals and groups to be willing to try anything that offers hope for advancing God's project.*

If we, as Christians, following the teachings of Jesus Christ, are committed to advancing God's evolutionary project, we will always be involved on the front lines in every field. Not all our efforts or projects, individual and collective, will be successful. Failure is to be expected. Moral weakness is to be afraid to try, or to play it safe, or to stay in the background.

Ethical Principle 4. *Two primary ethical responsibilities shared by every person and group are (1) to build and maintain an ever-expanding loving community among human beings, and (2) to care for the health and welfare of the planet (to love matter).*

Even though Christians, alone or in teams, would be committed to making advances in each field that affects evolution, they could never forget that everything they do is to be carried out in love, in service to building God's kingdom here on Earth. Therefore, the ultimate purpose of all our forward-thinking efforts is to foster healthy and loving communities.

Moral responsibility does not apply simply to individuals but to all groups, relationships, and organizations. Most events and activities are carried out within relationships and organizations. Morally, a group's actions are either involved in caring for humanity and Earth, or not. Morality from now on would mostly involve group morality.

In addition, all our discoveries in science, technology, art, and the like depend on the most basic forms of "matter" found on our planet. Everything we use to foster evolution, for example, automobiles, homes, or cell phones, are made of matter. Thus, caring for the welfare of the air, water, and other resources of the planet remains crucial. Living on a sick or dying planet keeps us from our God-given task to transform the world for God.

Ethical Principle 5. *In addition, each person and group, according to its resources of love-energy, is morally obliged to nurture the evolutionary process.*

You will notice very quickly that, among these ethical principles, there are no lists of personal sins named or even suggested, as one might find in a traditional moral theology textbook or a catechism. Teilhard is not denying that it is a breach of the moral law and a rejection of God's love to violate another's trust or reputation by lying, cheating, murdering, committing adultery, using physical and sexual abuse, and the rest.

In an evolutionary world, however, God's focus is not on our failures, our weaknesses, or our sins, but on the accomplishment of God's evolutionary project. God's interest is on the moral obligation inherent in each one's capacity to foster that divine project personally and in cooperation with others.

Ethical Principle 6. *Every person and group have many resources for nurturing the evolutionary process.*

Teilhard wants us to begin thinking more like our merciful God. He wants us to begin believing that even human beings who have "sinned" want to do good in the world. I suspect that Jesus saw many sinners, including some his own chosen twelve apostles, not as inherently evil but rather as weak, emotionally immature, or morally underdeveloped (unripe). Most of us are still morally underdeveloped.[12]

To help such underdeveloped people gain personal self-discipline, develop emotionally, and grow in moral consciousness remains a continually important work for God's project. If that is the kind of work you do, for example, when parenting, teaching, or counseling, you are doing a most important work in God's project. The hope is that, as we all mature emotionally and morally, we may contribute more directly and powerfully to the growth of the world in love.

Ethical Principle 7. *One's ethical obligations may change over time, depending on one's change in resources or level of spiritual growth.*

This principle is true also for groups; their obligations may change over time. Because we live in an evolving universe, these ethical principles are not rules, but principles to guide daily and long-range decisions and actions. They are not static or fixed. Their meaning and manner of application will change as we evolve, personally and collectively.

God is less concerned about your weaknesses and susceptibility to temptations. He is much more concerned about developing your ability to work with others in helping transform the world in ways only you can contribute.

Ethical Principle 8. *In an evolutionary ethic, personal sins are primarily sins of omission.*

Acts like murder and adultery may indeed hinder the progress of God's project. But for someone simply to claim that they have *not* committed murder, adultery, or sexual abuse accomplishes nothing positive to promote God's project. Such avoidance of sin or adherence to the rules of traditional good moral behavior may give one a feeling of self-righteousness. But that feeling does not necessarily produce growth in the kingdom of God. Positive action and effort are required.

Suppose, for example, that God's project was to build a house and you were a roofing expert. In an evolutive morality, you would stay focused on using your talents to help build the roof of God's house. Getting God's house built should be your most important moral concern. You may have weaknesses and failures in certain areas of your life. So does everyone. We are all weak and immature finite creatures, and we strive to improve ourselves. But in this ethical approach, doing your "roofing work" is your primary moral and ethical responsibility.[13]

Ethical Principle 9. *A major purpose for acts of healing, forgiveness, and mercy toward the sick, grieving, rejected, orphans, widows, the unemployed, anyone vulnerable or in need is to enable recipients of our care to rejoin the community so that they may make their unique loving contribution to God's project.*

The evolutionary viewpoint says that these often forgotten and summarily dismissed people may have gifts and abilities to further humanity's growth in consciousness and compassion. They need to be given the chance to make their unique contributions. The best way to make this possible is to help them rejoin community life as productive members.

Teilhard's moral principles apply to all human beings and all groups of people, no matter what their religion or lack of it.[14] Everyone is involved; everyone is called.

Evolution and Suffering

91. Can suffering contribute to God's evolutionary project?

Once, someone asked Teilhard to write on the meaning of suffering. Near the end of his essay, titled "The Meaning and Constructive Value of Suffering," he wrote these astounding words:

> Human suffering, the sum total of suffering poured out at each moment over the whole earth, is like an immeasurable ocean. But what makes up this immensity? Is it blackness, emptiness, barren wastes? No, indeed: it is potential energy. Suffering holds hidden within it, in extreme intensity, the ascensional force of the world.
>
> The whole point is to set this force free by making it conscious of what it signifies and of what it is capable. For if all the sick people in the world were simultaneously to turn their sufferings into a single shared longing for the speedy completion of the kingdom of God through the organizing of the earth, what a vast leap toward God the world would thereby make![15]

92. How does Teilhard explain his belief about the value of suffering?

Teilhard realized that suffering often requires the expenditure of tremendous amounts of energy. Christ expended tremendous amounts of physical energy during his passion and especially during his hours on the cross. But he didn't waste that energy. He directed the energy of his suffering for two powerful purposes: first, to accomplish the forgiveness of humanity's sins for all times and, second, to energize human beings for all future times to help achieve God's project in the world.[16]

Many people are unaware of this second purpose of Christ's suffering energy. But it is this second energy in which we participate as we use our human energy to work at our individual and group contributions to God's project.

Teilhard realized that human beings could similarly direct the energy of their suffering by sharing in Christ's second purpose, namely, by directing that energy by their intention toward the success of some part of God's project.

St. Paul recognized and actively participated in Christ's second, and perhaps larger, purpose of suffering on the cross, when he wrote to his community, "I am now rejoicing in my sufferings for your sake, and in my flesh I am completing what is lacking in Christ's afflictions for the sake of his body, that is, the church" (Col 1:24).

Paul's suffering—and ours, too—cannot be dedicated to the "expiation of sin" purpose of Christ's suffering, that is, for the forgiveness of our sins. Only Christ could fulfill that purpose. But the second purpose of Christ's suffering, bringing his cosmic Body to maturity, is something to which Paul and all of us can contribute. "It is he whom we proclaim, warning everyone and teaching everyone in all wisdom, so that we may present everyone mature in Christ. For this I toil and struggle with all the energy that he powerfully inspires within me" (Col 1:28–29).

93. How do many Christians view human suffering today?

Many Christians today view human suffering as a useless waste of energy. However, the energy of suffering can also be consciously directed as a force for good. The church could teach all suffering people to realize how, by their conscious intention, they could use their suffering to help produce a transformation of the world. The energy spent in all forms of human suffering, not merely physical pain but also emotional and spiritual pain, may be consciously directed to the success of God's project.

Thus, God's project could be moved forward in two ways: First, by our conscious actions to promote betterment and, second, by the way we consciously focus the energy we spend in suffering or enduring the difficulties we face in life.

In the book *Teilhard de Chardin: Seven Stages of Suffering*, there are many suggestions on how to use suffering to help improve the world. It describes spiritual practices for those who must endure suffering.

What Can We Do?

94. Who should be involved in God's project?

God has a plan or project to be carried out on Earth and God invites all human beings and groups to cooperate in this work.[17] God has planted within every person the drive to make a positive difference in the world.[18] It follows that every human being has an active role to play in this work. God is not calling merely clergy and vowed religious people to help renew the face of Earth, but everyone, especially laypeople, even nonbelievers and atheists. God has implanted the desire to do good into every human mind and heart.

95. Are atheists involved in God's plan and project?

Scores of famous men and women in science and technology—biologists, physicists, anthropologists, astronomers, chemists, physicians, and mathematicians—have publicly identified themselves as atheists. In fact, their atheism, or rejection of traditional religion, may have even influenced their notable activities or contributions to public life—and to human evolution. Many Nobel Prize winners or recipients of other humanitarian and scientific awards are atheists. Among them are quantum physicist Niels Bohr; biologist Francis Crick, who codiscovered the structure of the DNA molecule; psychologist Albert Ellis; quantum mechanics scientist Richard Feynman; psychoanalyst Sigmund Freud; psychologist Erich Fromm; mathematician and physicist Stephen Hawking; physicist Peter Higgs, known for his prediction of the existence of a new particle, the Higgs boson, ironically nicknamed the "God particle"; chemist Linus Pauling, recipient of the Nobel Peace Prize; mathematical physicist Roger Penrose, whose formulas enable many astronomical calculations; analytic philosopher Bertrand Russell; neurologist and famous author Oliver Sachs; computer inventor Alan Turing; biologist Craig Venter, one of the first researchers to sequence the human genome; and chemist James Watson, codiscoverer of the DNA.

It is not required that individuals consciously know that they are helping God's project move toward its fulfillment, only that they carry out their purpose in life. God's invitation is written in each person's heart as well as in their genes, their experiences, and their culture.

96. What can I do personally?

Reflect on this question with an open heart, an open imagination, an open mind. Be open to the ways that the future of Christianity could be influenced.

Today, most evolutionary steps occur through teamwork. If you listen to the Holy Spirit, you will be drawn toward others who are looking for an opportunity to serve God's evolutionary project. At first, the thought of getting involved in something outside of your normal "box" may frighten or repel you. But when you let the Spirit guide you, your involvement will become a source of great joy—one of the richest blessings of your life. Psychologist Bill Plotkin says, "You need to find what is genuinely yours to offer the world before you can make it a better place. What are you passionate and enthusiastic about? What or who inspires you? Discovering your unique gift to bring to your community is your greatest opportunity and challenge. The offering of that gift—your true self—is the most you can do to love and serve the world. And it is all the world needs."[19]

When we develop a diversity of paths and a more expansive vision of action, the human journey toward unity becomes more robust, more beautiful. All of us play our parts in the evolving, universe-spanning Christ Mystery.

97. How will this evolutionary attitude affect my prayer life?

From your prayer, you will be able to understand more clearly what work is yours to do and find the courage to do it. The "soul" part of you already knows, desires, and truly seeks God's will. Discernment of God's will comes naturally to you in prayer because, in that vision, "I" and God appear to be one. In this way, God's grace becomes a human attribute, which confirms goodness, peace, and happiness. Thus, the essential realization is that grace is shareable. The virtue of grace is given to us by God as both a gift and a responsibility. Franciscan priest and writer Richard Rohr states:

> The power of the biblical proclamation is that it clearly invites us into "cooperation" (Romans 8:28), free "participation" (Philippians 3:10), and the love of free and mature persons in God (Ephesians 4:13). We can apparently trust ourselves to grow because God has done it first and foremost throughout cosmic history and especially with the human species. The Christ we are asking for and waiting for includes our own full birth and the further birth of history and creation. Now we can say, "Come, Christ Jesus" with a whole new understanding and a deliberate passion![20]

Evolutionary thinking leaves the future of humanity and the planet in God's hands. Evolutive workers struggle to do what they can to promote human unity and simultaneously, in prayer, humbly accept what they only tentatively know.

98. What are some specific results or accomplishments needed to foster the kind of evolution that brings about harmony, peace, and unanimity among various people living on the planet?

Here are a few suggestions.

- *Peace academies.* Every nation has its military academies where men and women are trained in warfare, for example, in the United States, we have West Point and the Naval Academy at Annapolis, and several others. Few if any of the world's nations have a corresponding Peace Academy, where men and women are trained and dedicated to study the art of peacemaking, diplomacy, compromise, and collaboration.
- *Nondual thinking.* Our education system teaches only dualistic thinking (Aristotle's mode). "A thing is either this or that. A is A and B is B. A cannot be A and B at the same time." As long as dualistic thinking remains the only way we do human reasoning, we can never achieve a peaceful planet. It is not a matter of listing similarities and differences and saying that our similarities outweigh our differences. Nondual thinking embraces entire ways of thinking and perceiving that may be different from our accustomed way of thinking.

  Dualism also spawns the "we-they" mentality that divides us into "good people/bad people" and allows us to demonize the adversary. Dualism is the root of authoritarian and entitlement behavior. It generates racism and makes conflicts and wars inevitable.
- *Laws of evolution.* Everyone, beginning in childhood, needs to learn the principles and laws of evolution and how to use them in practical ways. One might say that such teaching could be part of a Christian catechism. This would include training in how to form "symbiotic" relationships and how to function in teams.

- *Cooperative games and sports.* Competition—winning vs. losing—is a dominant value in contemporary human society. It pervades business, sports, and education. All of these dimensions of life confirm the unchallenged value of competition. Unfortunately, although competition has its role in human society, it ultimately prevents the achievement of true human unity. Development of cooperative games, where everyone wins, could help bring a balance to the universal penchant for competition and foster an alternative vision of human potential.

99. What is "evolutionary thinking"?

According to Richard Rohr,

> Evolutionary thinking is, for me, the very core concept of faith, where we trust that God alone steers this mysterious universe, where there is clearly much hidden from us and much still before us—and where "eye has not seen, and ear has not heard, and the human heart has not conceived, what God has prepared for those who love God" (1 Cor 2:9).
>
> Evolutionary thinking is contemplative thinking. It leaves the full field of the future in God's hands and agrees to humbly hold the present with what it only tentatively knows for sure.
>
> Evolutionary thinking agrees to knowing and not knowing *simultaneously*. It sends us on a trajectory, where the ride is itself the destination, and the goal is never clearly in sight. To stay on the ride, to trust the trajectory, to know it is moving, and moving somewhere always better, is just another way to describe faith. We are all in evolution all the time.[21]

We must suffer through the present to reach something higher, something more unified, more conscious, more being in love. Hope must be born over and over again, for where there is love, there is hope. Christian life is birthing love into greater unity; it is our contribution to a universe in evolution. We point the way to something more than ourselves, something up ahead that we are now participating in, where heaven and earth will be renewed (Revelation 21).[22]

100. Why would I want to become an evolutive (Catholic) Christian?

We now know that our loving God created an evolving universe, and that God, in divine self-expression, implanted that creative love in every particle of the universe. That implanted love causes us to be attracted to each other and to other things, and to form loving bonds with them—with people, animals, and nature itself. The law of love is active in the bones and blood of every creature.

Evolution today is happening primarily in the realms of mind and heart. Witness the technical and scientific innovations happening today in medicine, health care, communication, ecology, space exploration, and a growing sense of caring for our planet.

Evolution is also happening in religion. God's love is driving us to find ways for different religions to be attracted to one another, not to convert one another, but to celebrate the different pathways God has provided for finding God and ways to enrich each other.

In this way, life and love spread and evolve all over the earth. Evolution is clearly aiming toward creating one loving human family. Achieving that oneness in love still has a long way to go. We are still working on it. God is the divine project manager, guiding it.

Because this is the case, Christians should be more excited about the discoveries of science than anyone else. For such discoveries clarify for us more about God's nature, God's ways, and God's purpose in creating the universe. In many ways, research scientists are continuing to light God's "lamp" to reveal the mysteries of creation.

Christian theology more openly understood gives evolution its meaning and purpose. It offers a way to guide evolution's direction. It offers the insight that love—divine love and human love—is the driving force moving evolution forward.

You are invited to take an active part in this evolutionary momentum.

101. Is it time for a new and expanded understanding of our covenant with God?

Yes, because humanity keeps evolving in its self-understanding, its understanding of the universe, and its understanding of God.

The great themes of the New Testament built on those of the Old Testament and went beyond them. Similarly, the new covenant between God and humanity goes beyond the old covenant between God and the Hebrew people. It signifies a new relationship between God and humanity.

God has not changed; it is humanity that has changed. Thanks in great part to Christian developments in philosophy and science, the human family has grown in its self-understanding in ways that enable people to see God no longer as a tribal God but as a God who lovingly embraces all people.

Humanity didn't stop growing and developing in the first century. We have continued to evolve in our understanding of our place within the life of our planet and the vast universe in which we live. In a new development of human consciousness, especially in the discoveries of science, we have come to realize that everything in the universe has been evolving, that is, becoming something new that was never here before.

Two centuries ago, no one believed or imagined that we human beings are an evolving species that live on an ever-evolving planet in an ever-evolving universe. Since we now know that evolution permeates all dimensions of existence, we must acknowledge that God created not the fixed and perfect universe we had assumed but an evolving and perfectible one.

As humanity has developed in its self-understanding in new ways, we are enabled to see God and the teachings of Jesus in new ways. We now see God as the Evolver, the one who lovingly is always making things new. "And the one who was seated on the [heavenly] throne said, 'See, I am making all things new.' Also he said, 'Write this down, for these words are trustworthy and true'" (Rev 21:5).

Because of our awareness of evolution, we are able to have a new level of understanding of this divine revelation. It calls for a new understanding of the covenant between God and humanity, one that challenges us human beings to use our efforts in continually evolving our ever-perfectible humanity and caring for the planet that supports us.

Notes

Part 1

1. Ilia Delio, *The Emergent Christ* (Maryknoll, NY: Orbis Books, 2011), 22.

2. Pius XII, *Humani Generis* (August 12, 1950), https://www.vatican.va/content/pius-xii/en/encyclicals/documents/hf_p-xii_enc_12081950_humani-generis.html, 36.

3. Philip Pullella, "Evolution Fine but No Apology to Darwin: Vatican," September 16, 2008, https://www.reuters.com/article/us-vatican-evolution/evolution-fine-but-no-apology-to-darwin-vatican-idUSLG62672220080916.

4. Wikipedia, "Theistic Evolution," https://en.wikipedia.org/wiki/Theistic_evolution.

5. Francis S. Collins, *The Language of God: A Scientist Presents Evidence for Belief* (New York: Free Press, 2007), 200.

6. Claude E. Stipe, "Scientific Creationism and Evangelical Christianity," *American Anthropologist* New Series 87, no. 1 (March 1985): 149. See also Eugenie C. Scott, "Antievolution and Creationism in the United States," *Annual Review of Anthropology* 26 (1997): 263–89.

7. To be precise, the adjective *evolutionary* is found at least once. Pope Paul VI, "Introductory Statement," *Gaudium et Spes, Pastoral Constitution on the Church in the Modern World* (December 7, 1965), 5.

8. Among the documents of Vatican II, the *Pastoral Constitution on the Church in the Modern World* (*Gaudium et Spes*) is perhaps the most forward-looking document produced by the Council. Much of the material in Chapter 2, Section 3, paragraph 62, of this document was most likely inspired by Teilhard de Chardin, according to footnote no. 11, in Walter Abbott, ed., *The Documents of Vatican II* (New York: MacMillan, 1966), 204.

9. John Paul II, Message to the Participants in the Plenary of the Pontifical Academy of Sciences, 22 October 1996, https://www.vatican.va/content/john-paul-ii/it/messages/pont_messages/1996/documents/hf_jp-ii_mes_19961022_evoluzione.html.

10. John Paul II, Message to the Pontifical Academy of Sciences, 22 October 1996.

11. John Paul II, Message to the Pontifical Academy of Sciences, 22 October 1996.

12. Pope Francis, On the Occasion of the Inauguration of the Bust in Honour of Pope Benedict XVI, 28 October 2014, https://www.vatican.va/content/francesco/en/speeches/2014/october/documents/papa-francesco_20141027_plenaria-accademia-scienze.html.

13. *Catechism of the Catholic Church*, 2nd ed. (Washington, DC: United States Catholic Conference of Bishops, 2011), 302.

14. *Catechism*, 283.

15. *Catechism*, 283.

16. Pullella, "Evolution Fine."

17. "Galileo vs. the Catholic Church," https://www.lee.k12.nc.us/cms/lib03/NC01001912/Centricity/Domain/1464/Galileo.pdf.

18. For a complete text of *Pascendi Dominici Gregis*, see https://www.vatican.va/content/pius-x/en/encyclicals/documents/hf_p-x_enc_19070908_pascendi-dominici-gregis.html.

19. For a complete text of the Oath, see https://www.papalencyclicals.net/pius10/p10moath.htm.

20. Wikipedia, "Creationism," https://en.wikipedia.org/wiki/Creationism.

21. Wikipedia, "Creationism."

22. Data from Harriet Zuckerman, *Scientific Elite: Nobel Laureates in the United States* (New York: The Free Press, 1977); Baruch A. Shalev, *100+ Years of Nobel Prizes and More.* The Americas Group, updated archive November 2020. See also "All Nobel Prizes" in The Nobel Foundation: Archived: from the original on June 15, 2020.

23. See Louis M. Savary, *The Christian Phenomenon: A Once and Future Church; The Vision of Teilhard de Chardin* (Mahwah, NJ: Paulist Press, 2024).

24. Much of the following material was adapted from Joseph Liu, "Religious Groups' Views on Evolution," February 3, 2014, https://www.pewresearch.org/religion/2009/02/04/religious-groups-views-on-evolution/.

25. The Episcopal Church Network for Science, Technology and Faith, *A Catechism of Creation*, "Part II: Creation and Science," 8–15,

https://www.episcopalchurch.org/wp-content/uploads/sites/2/2021/03/CC-CreationCatechism.pdf.

26. Evangelical Lutheran Church in America, "Ask a Scientist: Questions and Answers about Faith and Science," https://download.elca.org/ELCA%20Resource%20Repository/faithandscience_askascientist.pdf.

27. Lutheran Church–Missouri Synod, *Doctrinal Positions of the LCMS*, "Of Creation," https://www.lcms.org/about/beliefs/doctrine/brief-statement-of-lcms-doctrinal-position#creation.

28. Answersingenesis.org, "'No Contradiction' between Evolution and Bible—PCUSA," https://answersingenesis.org/theistic-evolution/god-and-evolution/no-contradiction-between-evolution-and-bible-pcusa/.

29. Presbyterian Church (U.S.A.), "The Dialogue between Science and Faith," March 16, 2020, https://www.presbyterianmission.org/resource/paper-dialogue-between-science-and-faith/.

30. United Methodist Church, "Social Principles: The Natural World," The Book of Discipline of The United Methodist Church, 2016, https://www.umc.org/en/content/social-principles-the-natural-world#science-tech.

31. United Church of Christ, "A New Voice Arising: A Pastoral Letter on Faith Engaging Science and Technology," January 2008, https://www.ucc.org/wp-content/uploads/2021/01/pastoral-letter-on-faith-and-science.pdf.

32. Southern Baptist Convention, "Resolution on Scientific Creationism," *SBC Resolutions*, June 1, 1982, https://www.sbc.net/resource-library/resolutions/resolution-on-scientific-creationism/.

33. The unpronounced divine Hebrew name YHWH, four consonants, is sometimes rendered into English and German translations as either "Yahweh" or "Jehovah," depending on the vowels chosen to render the four consonants pronounceable. Since Germans prefer Jehovah and since German biblical scholars were first to identify the four editorial groups, they chose to use *J* to indicate the Yahwist editors.

Part 2

1. Richard Rohr, *The Universal Christ: How a Forgotten Reality Can Change Everything We See, Hope For, and Believe* (Colorado Springs, CO: Convergent Books, 2019), 96.

2. Helena Curtis and N. Sue Barnes, *Biology*, 5th ed. (New York: Worth Publishers, 1989), 974.

3. Ed Grabianowski, "How Symbiosis Works," HowStuffWorks, https://science.howstuffworks.com/life/evolution/symbiosis.htm?utm_source=howstuffworks&utm_medium=recirc.

4. Teilhard was not the first to recognize the reality of a relationship. Thomas Aquinas stated it clearly almost a thousand years before. He said, *Relatio est realis.* (A relationship is something real or has its own existence.)

5. John Paul II, Message to the Participants in the Plenary of the Pontifical Academy of Sciences, October 22, 1996, https://www.vatican.va/content/john-paul-ii/it/messages/pont_messages/1996/documents/hf_jp-ii_mes_19961022_evoluzione.html, 4.

6. Denise Schmandt-Besserat, "The Evolution of Writing," in *International Encyclopedia of Social and Behavioral Sciences*, ed. James Wright (Amsterdam: Elsevier, 2014), https://sites.utexas.edu/dsb/tokens/the-evolution-of-writing/#:~:text=The%20cuneiform%20script%2C%20created%20in,recording%20goods%20with%20clay%20tokens.

7. *Evolutive* describes individuals, groups, or organizations that, in their values and actions, are committed to promoting the evolutionary progress of the human race.

Part 3

1. Pierre Teilhard de Chardin, *The Human Phenomenon*, trans. Sarah Appleton-Weber (Portland, OR: Sussex Academic Press, 2002), 192.

2. Thomas Woods Jr., "Review of Paul Legutko's *How the Catholic Church Built Western Civilization*," National Review Book Service, August 22, 2006.

3. Woods, review of *How the Catholic Church Built Western Civilization*. More recently, Matthew Gabrielle and David M. Perry's book, *The Bright Ages* (New York: Harper, 2022), described the Middle Ages as the times when the Catholic Church drove scientific progress and art.

4. Karl Heussi, *Kompendium der Kirchengeschichte, 11* (Tübingen, Germany: Auflage, 1956), 317–19, 325–26.

5. Although Roman Catholic women, even today, remain excluded from the clerical state, they manage many of the details of parish community life, education, and worship as well as serve in key positions of

ecclesiastical influence. Some have suggested that the Catholic hierarchy remains one of the last bastions of male privilege and supremacy.

6. Timothy Miller, "The Birth of the Hospital in the Byzantine Empire," *The Henry E. Sigerist Supplements to the Bulletin of the History of Medicine* 10 (1985): 142–46. PubMed ID 3902734.

7. Miller, "Birth of the Hospital," 142–46.

8. Geoffrey Blainey, *A Short History of Christianity* (New York: Viking, 2011), 214–15.

9. John Agnew, "*Deus Vult*: The Geopolitics of Catholic Church," *Geopolitics* 15, no. 1 (12 February 2010): 39–61.

10. Roy Gardner, Denis Lawton, and Jo Cairns, *Faith Schools* (London: Routledge, 2005), 148.

11. Daniel Kennedy, "St. Albertus Magnus," *The Catholic Encyclopedia*, vol 1 (New York: Appleton, 1907).

12. Gardner, Lawton, and Cairns, *Faith Schools*, 148.

13. United States Catholic Conference of Bishops, "Catholic Education," https://www.usccb.org/offices/public-affairs/catholic-education.

14. Pierre Teilhard de Chardin, *The Future of Man*, trans. Norman Denny (New York: Harper & Row, 1964), 32.

15. This is the general thrust of the book by Michael J. Murray, Michael Rea, and Edward N. Zalta, *Philosophy and Christian Theology* (Stanford, CA: Metaphysics Research Lab, Stanford University, 2016).

16. These include Clement of Alexandria (150–215), Origen of Alexandria (184–253), Athanasius of Alexandria (296–373), Gregory Nazianzus (329–90), Gregory of Nyssa (335–95), Ambrose (340–97), John Chrysosotom (347–407), Augustine of Hippo (354–430), Cyril of Alexandria (378–444), and Boethius (477–524).

17. These include Isadore of Seville (540–604), Bede (672–735), Radbertus (785–865), Anselm of Canterbury (1033–1109), Peter Abelard (1079–1142), Bernard of Clairvaux (1090–1153), Peter Lombard (1096–1160), and Hildegard of Bingen (1098–1179).

18. These include Albertus Magnus (1193–1280), Roger Bacon (1219–92), Bonaventure (1221–74), Thomas Aquinas (1225–74), Meister Eckhart (1260–1328), John Duns Scotus (1266–1308), William of Ockham (1287–1333), Jean Buridan (1300–58), Bridget of Sweden (1303–73), Nicole Oresme (1325–82), Catherine of Sienna (1347–80), Jean Gerson (1363–1429), and Nicholas of Cusa (1401–64).

19. Jorge J. E. Gracia, quoted in Nicholas Bunnin and E. P. Tsui-James, eds., *The Blackwell Companion to Philosophy*, 2nd ed. (Hoboken, NJ: Blackwell, 2002), 1.

20. These include Joseph de Maistre (1753–1821), John Henry Newman (1801–90), Henri Lacordaire (1802–61), Orestes Brownson (1803–76), Alexis de Tocqueville (1805–59), Frederick William Faber (1814–63), Gregor Mendel (1822–84), Henry Oxenham (1829–88), Vladimir Soloviev (1853–1900), Maurice Blondel (1861–1949), Henri Brémond (1865–1933), Paul Claudel (1868–1955), Hilaire Belloc (1870–1953), Charles Peguy (1873–1914), G. K. Chesterton (1874–1936), Max Scheler (1874–1928), Reginald Garrigou-Lagrange (1877–1964), Pierre Teilhard de Chardin (1881–1955), Jacques Maritain (1882–1973), Etienne Gilson (1884–1978), Christopher Dawson (1889–1970), Gabriel Marcel (1889–1973), Martin Heidegger (1889–1976), Dietrich von Hildebrand (1889–1977), Edith Stein (1891–1942), and Henri de Lubac (1896–1991).

21. These include Mortimer Adler (1902–2001), Josef Pieper (1904–97), John Courtney Murray (1904–67), Karl Rahner (1904–84), Yves Congar (1904–95), Bernard Lonergan (1904–84), Jean Danielou (1905–74), Emmanuel Mounier (1905–50), Hans Urs von Balthasar (1905–68), Fredrick Copleston (1907–94), Marshall McLuhan (1911–80), Walter J. Ong (1912–2003), Edward Schillebeeckx (1914–2009), Thomas Berry (1914–2009), W. Norris Clarke (1915–2008), Thomas Merton (1915–68), Avery Dulles (1918–2008), Karol Wojtyla (1920–2005), René Girard (1923–2015), Juan Luis Secundo (1925–96), Ivan Illich (1926–2002), Joseph Ratzinger (1927–2022), Raymond Brown (1928–98), Mary Daly (1928–2010), Hans Küng (1928–2021), Joan Chittister (1936–), Leonardo Boff (1938–), Jon Sobrino (1938–), Elizabeth Schüssler Fiorenza (1938–), David Tracy (1939–), and Elizabeth A. Johnson (1941–).

22. "Illuminated Manuscripts and How They Were Created," Park West Gallery (October 23, 2017), https://www.parkwestgallery.com/what-are-illuminated-manuscripts-and-how-were-they-created/.

23. Wikipedia.org, "Stained Glass," https://en.wikipedia.org/wiki/Stained_glass.

24. Discovered by Italian Renaissance architect, Filippo Brunelleschi (1377–1446). "Filippo Brunelleschi," https://www.wikiart.org/en/filippo-brunelleschi.

25. Wikipedia.org, "Perspective (Graphical)," https://en.wikipedia.org/wiki/Perspective_(graphical).

26. Wikipedia.org, "Jan van Eyck," https://en.wikipedia.org/wiki/Jan_van_Eyck.

27. Isidore of Seville, *The Etymologies of Isidore of Seville*, trans. with introduction and notes by Stephen A. Barney, W. J. Lewis, J. A. Beach, and Oliver Berghof (Cambridge: Cambridge University Press, 2006), 95.

28. Guido also invented the verbal symbols to denote the eight notes of the major scale: *Do, Re Mi, Fa, Sol, La, Ti, Do.*

29. The earliest evidence for their existence may be found in paintings by Gaudenzio Ferrari from the 1530s, though Ferrari's instruments had only three strings.

30. The best-known maker of the English slide trumpet, Kohler (London), began making instruments with three piston valves, patented by John Bayley in 1862: the Handel Trumpet (in F) and Acoustic Cornet (in Bb). Michael Calore, "May 3, 1815: Blown Away by Horn with Valves," Wired.com (May 3, 2018), https://www.wired.com/2010/05/0503brass-valve-horns/#:~.

31. Stanley L. Jaki, *The Savior of Science* (Grand Rapids: Eerdmans, 2000), 2.

32. David C. Lindberg and Ronald L. Numbers, introduction to *God & Nature: Historical Essays on the Encounter between Christianity and Science* (Berkeley: University of California Press, 1986), 5–12.

33. Material and quotations in this paragraph and the next can be found in Thomas Woods Jr., *How the Catholic Church Built Western Civilization* (New York: Regnery, 2005).

34. For a complete text of *Pascendi,* see https:// www.vatican.va/content/pius-x/en/encyclicals/documents/hf_p-x_enc_19070908_pascendi-dominici-gregis.html.

35. For a complete text of the Oath, see https:// www.papalencyclicals.net/pius10/p10moath.htm.

36. The requirement for taking this oath was in effect from 1910 until 1967.

37. Pierre Teilhard de Chardin, *Christianity and Evolution: Reflections on Science and Religion*, trans. René Hague (Boston: Houghton Mifflin Harcourt, 1969), 199.

Part 4

1. Richard Rohr, *The Universal Christ: How a Forgotten Reality Can Change Everything We See, Hope For, and Believe* (Colorado Springs, CO: Convergent Books, 2019), 95.

2. Pierre Teilhard de Chardin, *The Human Phenomenon*, trans. Sarah Appleton-Weber (Portland, OR: Sussex Academic Press, 2003), 214.

3. *Evolutive* describes individuals, groups, or organizations that, in their values and actions, are committed to promoting the evolutionary progress of the human race.

4. Pierre Teilhard de Chardin, *The Future of Man*, trans. Norman Denny (New York: Harper & Row, 1964), 32.

5. Teilhard de Chardin, *Phenomenon,* 213.

6. Pierre Teilhard de Chardin, *Human Energy*, trans. J. M. Cohen (New York: Harcourt Brace Jovanovich, 1969), 44.

7. Ursula King, *Teilhard de Chardin and Eastern Religions: Spirituality and Mysticism in an Evolutionary World* (Mahwah, NJ: Paulist Press, 2011), 179.

8. King, *Teilhard de Chardin and Eastern Religions,* 179–80.

9. See Louis Savary, *Teilhard de Chardin on Morality: Living in an Evolving World* (Mahwah, NJ: Paulist Press, 2019) for a fuller discussion of these moral and ethical principles.

10. St. Paul is very clear on the spiritual gifts, especially love. Among the gifts given to everyone, love is the greatest. "[Love] bears all things, believes all things, hopes all things, endures all things" (1 Cor 13:7). Or, in another translation of the same verse, "There is nothing love cannot face; there is no limit to its faith, its hope, and its endurance" (*New English Bible with Apocrypha* [Oxford University Press, 1970]).

11. St. Paul's opinion is very clear on those who are not using their gifts to nurture the community. "For even when we were with you, we gave you this command: Anyone unwilling to work should not eat. For we hear that some of you are living in idleness, mere busybodies, not doing any work. Now such persons we command and exhort in the Lord Jesus Christ to do their work quietly and to earn their own living. Brothers and sisters, do not be weary in doing what is right" (2 Thess 3:10–13).

12. St. Paul treats his immature followers gently but firmly. See 1 Cor 3:1–9.

13. St. Paul expands on this idea of each one in the community, as members of Christ's Body, having different qualifications and different

works to perform. For example, he says, the work that the eyes do for the body is different from the work that the ears do, and the work of the hands and feet are different from the jobs of other body parts. Paul says, "God arranged the members in the body, each one of them, as he chose. If all were a single member, where would the body be? As it is, there are many members, yet one body" (1 Cor 12:18–20). And "If one member suffers, all suffer together with it; if one member is honored, all rejoice together with it" (1 Cor 12:26). Then, Paul talks about the various human gifts or talents given to each one in the community—to be an apostle, prophet, teacher, healer, etc. Each person has unique gifts, and no one person has every gift (12:28–31). However, everyone has the gifts of faith, hope, and love. These gifts are meant to be used in building the universal Body of Christ.

14. Although these principles are derived from Teilhard's Roman Catholic theological perspective and his vision of *Christogenesis*, I am sure he would prefer to see them formulated as they are here, in ways acceptable to all humans (*cosmogenesis*). However, in each case, I present their development from Teilhard's own Christian scriptural and theological perspective.

15. N. Braybrooke, ed., *Teilhard de Chardin: Pilgrim of the Future* (New York: Libra Books, 1964), 23–26.

16. Teilhard describes these two purposes as the "Cross of Expiation" and the "Cross of Evolution" in *Christianity and Evolution: Reflections on Science and Religion*, trans. René Hague (Boston: Houghton Mifflin Harcourt, 1969), 216–19. He notes that the institutional church in its liturgy and catechesis sometimes presents only the Cross of Expiation. St. Paul certainly saw both. See Col 1:24.

17. For Teilhard, the work of God's project cannot achieve its full strength without the participation of the different world faiths. See his essay "The Spirit of the Earth" in *Human Energy*, trans. J. M. Cohen (New York: Harcourt Brace Jovanovich, 1969), 19–47. For, as Ursula King says of the many living faith traditions, "they possess an ocean of energy reserves to help solve the problems of human action." She says we should seek to find: "What can the world's faiths contribute to the solution of contemporary problems such as attitudes towards money, unemployment, poverty, or war? What ethical insights do they possess to guide human action? What vision of God do they convey to draw us to higher spiritual ideals?" Ursula King, "Teilhard's Cosmic Spirituality" in *Rediscovering*

Teilhard's Fire, ed. Kathleen Duffy (Philadelphia: Saint Joseph's University Press, 2010), 19.

18. "I will put my law within them, and I will write it on their hearts; and I will be their God, and they shall be my people. No longer shall they teach one another, or say to each other, 'Know the Lord,' for they shall all know me, from the least of them to the greatest, says the Lord; for I will forgive their iniquity, and remember their sin no more" (Jer 31:33–34). Jeremiah doesn't exactly intend his message to be for the entire world, but one could easily extrapolate and apply the statement "I will put my law within them" universally. In our current understanding of God as Love, that "law" would be the law of love and, simultaneously, the law of evolution that Teilhard identified, the Law of Attraction-Connection-Complexity-Consciousness. Or, as Teilhard put it, "Without any doubt, there is hidden beneath the ascending movement of life, the continuous action of a being who raises up the universe from within" (Teilhard de Chardin, *Christianity and Evolution*, 29).

19. Bill Plotkin, quoted in Richard Rohr, "Seeking God's Will," *Daily Meditations* (blog), Center for Action and Contemplation, August 25, 2022, https://cac.org/daily-meditations/seeking-gods-will-2022-08-25/.

20. Richard Rohr, *The Universal Christ: How a Forgotten Reality Can Change Everything We See, Hope for, and Believe* (New York: Convergent, 2019), 20–21.

21. Adapted from Richard Rohr, "Evolution Is Another Name for Growth," *Oneing: Evolutionary Thinking* 4, no. 2 (Fall 2016): 112, 115–16.

22. Ilia Delio, *The Unbearable Wholeness of Being: God, Evolution, and the Power of Love* (Maryknoll, NY: Orbis Books, 2013), 198.

Recommended Reading

Delio, Ilia. *The Emergent Christ: Exploring the Meaning of Catholic in an Evolutionary Universe.* Maryknoll, NY: Orbis Books, 2011.

Haught, John F. *God after Darwin.* Boulder, CO: Westview Press, 2003.

———. *Responses to 101 Questions on God and Evolution.* Mahwah, NJ: Paulist Press, 2001.

Rohr, Richard. *The Universal Christ: How a Forgotten Reality Can Change Everything We See, Hope for, and Believe.* New York: Convergent Books, 2021.

Savary, Louis M. *Teilhard de Chardin's* The Phenomenon of Man *Explained.* Mahwah, NJ: Paulist Press, 2020.

Teilhard de Chardin, Pierre. *Christianity and Evolution.* Translated by René Hague. New York: Harcourt Brace, 1969.